W9-BTZ-856

COLLECTOR'S ENCYCLOPEDIA OF

FIESTA

EIGHTH EDITION

Plus Harlequin, Riviera, and Kitchen Kraft

Bob & Sharon Huxford

COLLECTOR BOOKS

A Division of Schroeder Publishing Co., Inc.

The current values in this book should be used only as a guide. They are not intended to set prices, which vary from one section of the country to another. Auction prices as well as dealer prices vary greatly and are affected by condition as well as demand. Neither the Authors nor the Publisher assumes responsibility for any losses that might be incurred as a result of consulting this guide.

Searching For A Publisher?

We are always looking for knowledgeable people considered to be experts within their fields. If you feel that there is a real need for a book on your collectible subject and have a large comprehensive collection, contact Collector Books.

On the Front Cover:

12" Fiesta Red Vase	$1,200.00+
13" Medium Green Chop Plate	$250.00 – 275.00
10" Yellow Dinner Plate	$28.00 – 32.00
Yellow Demitasse Pot	$320.00 – 340.00
Cobalt Carafe	$260.00 – 300.00
Ivory Bud Vase	$90.00 – 110.00
Dark Green Shaker	$20.00 – 22.00 each
Turquoise Sugar Bowl	$40.00 – 45.00
Green Demitasse Cup	$55.00 – 65.00
Fiesta Red Tripod Candle Holder	$275.00 – 300.00 each

On the Back Cover:

Bud Vase, in red cobalt, turquoise, and ivory	$90.00 – 110.00
Bud Vase, in yellow and light green	$70.00 – 80.00
8" Vase, in red cobalt, turquoise, and ivory	$600.00 – 700.00
8" Vase, in yellow and light green	$535.00 – 600.00
10" Vase, in red, cobalt, turquoise, and ivory	$780.00 – 850.00
10" Vase, in yellow and light green	$700.00 – 750.00
12" Vase, in red, cobalt, turquoise, and ivory	$1,200.00+
12" Vase, in yellow and light green	$1,000.00

Cover Design by Beth Summers
Book Design by Karen Smith

Additional copies of this book may be ordered from:

Collector Books
P.O. Box 3009
Paducah, Kentucky 42002-3009

@$19.95. Add $2.00 for postage and handling.

Copyright © 1998 by Sharon & Bob Huxford

All rights reserved. No part of this book may be reproduced, stored in any retrieval system, or transmitted in any form, or by any means including but not limited to electronic, mechanical, photocopying, recording, or otherwise, without the written consent of the authors and publisher.

Contents

Acknowledgments

If you have ever seen a copy of the first edition *Story of Fiesta*, you'll understand why we feel so overwhelmed when we face each new update. Granted, as soon as word got around that HLC was discontinuing Fiesta, it became an overnight sensation on the collectibles market, and from the start it was obvious that the ranks of Fiesta collectors were swelling day by day. But in the early '70s, all we needed or wanted were basic facts — what items could we expect to find and in what colors? So our first little paperback was a simple project. Bob and I had everything we needed to photograph for the book in our own collection, we were able to do all the basic research ourselves, and because we could easily sell all the extra pieces we could find, we knew just about what each item was worth. Over the years (twenty-four of them have passed since then), things have changed. "Fiesta" is basically now a household word. There are legions of collectors, some of them among the rich and famous! But today's collectors need to know details and lots of them! Their interests have branched in all directions. Prices have become so high that doing a value guide is a serious and demanding affair. Even if we were able to devote ourselves to this field entirely, we could no longer do it on our own, and of course, that we cannot do.

More than fifteen years ago, what started out as a hobby for us turned into a full-time business. As most of you probably know, we now edit many other books. Our interests have of necessity become very diversified. So we have invited collectors everywhere to help us keep abreast of the market, report and photograph new finds, take part in our price surveys, etc., and this they have done. So this is no longer a book by the Huxfords; this is a book by many, many collectors nationwide.

We especially want to thank those who took part in the price survey for this edition. These dealers and collectors are scattered throughout the entire country, and they are busy, busy people. Because of the scope of this book, the survey is lengthy and requires much of their time and a great amount of study. So to those who shared their knowledge and opinions with us, we send our thanks and appreciation.

In this edition you'll see many new photos. We've added about ninety, some of them are reshoots, others are of material you've never seen before. Some people have sent single photos, others have sent several, and we want you to know that each and every one was important to this book and was appreciated very much. As we began to lay out this edition and started adding the new photos, we included photo credits, but the farther we went with it, the more unfair it seemed to the (now anonymous) good people who supplied photos for our previous editions. We have simply included these new names in the list below. If we've disappointed anyone by omitting photo credits, we apologize. At the suggestion of one of our pricing team, we have also merged the names of contributors from the sixth and seventh editions with those who helped on this edition, since in many instances, the material they originally provided has been retained and remains a significant contribution.

There are people we want to specifically mention who deserve special credit for their participation, though we really do dread to start listing names for fear that we will inadvertently pass someone over. If your name does not appear in these acknowledgements and it should have, please forgive us. There are more than one-hundred-fifty people mentioned here, and we've tried very hard not to let a name slip by us. There are a few people, however, who must be recognized for going that extra mile.

Mick and Lorna Chase (Fiesta Plus) called and offered to put at our disposal a collection they had just purchased — one of the best and most complete in the country. They packed box after box of wonderful pieces, drove up from Cookeville, Tennessee, and met us in Paducah, where their newly acquired treasures were photographed by one of the country's finest photographers, Richard Walker, assisted by his wife Zibby, and Collector Books' in-house photographer, Charley Lynch. These photographs are the focal point of this edition, and we're sure you'll enjoy them tremendously. Few collectors have ever before had the opportunity to view vases in every size and color, all the AD coffeepots, all the regular coffeepots, all covered onion soups, and the many other spectacular items we photographed that day. To Lisa Stroup and everyone else who was involved in that shoot, we send thanks from the bottom of our hearts.

About twenty-five new photos are credited to Terry Telford, John Moses, Gus Gustafson, and Mike Haas, who got together with photographer Dave Prichard (Gray Barn Photography) and produced some great new shots of Kitchen Kraft, experimentals, Amberstone, Rhythm, Jubilee, and the Mexican lines as well as others. In addition to the photos, they also contributed information on these lines.

New Fiesta has become the object of much interest, and for keeping us up to date and informed on the new line, we must thank Joel Wilson. Not only did he send us the entire chapter (thoroughly organized), but he provided us with nearly all the photographs. Rod Wilson and Dave Beck also contributed to this chapter.

Mark Rumbolo was willing to shoot and reshoot his medium green Harlequin, and we appreciate all his efforts. Ray Vlach sent photos of the very early lines (Holland, Dreamland, etc.) as well as shots of children's dishes, Mexicana, Swing, and Century rarities. Jack and Treva Hamlin are to be commended for providing photos and text for such lines as Dogwood, Virginia Rose, and Priscilla. Please bear in mind that everyone whose name we mentioned above has contributed to the photography in this edition. There were others in past editions whose contributions were equally important and appreciated.

There is someone else we wouldn't think of omitting from the acknowledgments page, our late friend Austin Wilson. Austin and his wife Lucille came all the way to Indiana from Christiana, Pennsylvania, bringing hundreds of items from their personal collection to the Donahue Studios in Evansville to be photographed for the sixth edition, our first hardback. The Wilsons were avid collectors, very knowledgeable, and more than willing to share that knowledge with anyone who had questions. Many of those photos were used in this edition and serve in our minds as a memorial to a good friend and fellow collector.

We extend our thanks to the Homer Laughlin China Company for their continued cooperation and to our contacts there over the years, Ed Carson (now retired) and (presently) Dave Conley.

Thanks to all our readers who continue to correspond with us, sharing information, sending photographs, and keeping us up to date with timely news from the Fiesta "front." And thanks to all of you who buy our book, edition after edition, and still want more! God bless you all!

Don and Pat Adlesperger
Joe and Char Alexander
Millie Allen
Adam Anik
Mary Apgar
Philip Azeredo
Christina Baglivi
Mike Bainter
Sandra and Tim Baldwin
Jerry Barberio
Rita Barg
Dave Beck
Gary Beegle
Michael and Lisa Belcher
 (Sit-a-Spell Antiques)
Deane Bergsrud
Dennis Bialek
Donald G. Biellier
Ida Bonner
Dave Bowers
Robert Bowers
Kristen Bowman
Dennis Boyd
Paul Brache
Noel and Jennifer Brodzinski
Joyce Brooks
Ken Brown
Sharon C. Browning
Patrick Bunetta
Gloria and George Burkos
Dave Burrows
Jim Campbell
Tom Chanelli

Mick and Lorna Chase (Fiesta Plus)
Emily Chipps
Phillip and Joyce Clover
Don and Gail Contrell
Doug Dann
Chuck and Margaret Denlinger
 (Dancing Girl)
Carolyn Dock
Mike Drollinger
Robin and Bud Fennema
Darcy Fitspatrick
Steven P. Fonder
Terry Franks
Kathy Garrels
Jo Ann Giovannelli
Leona Gonzales
Robert Green
William and Donna Griglock
Gus Gustafson
 (chromatics@Buttzville Center)
Mike Haas
 (chromatics@Buttzville Center)
Jack and Treva Hamlin
David Hanrahan
Ted Haun
Mark Hoaglin
Margaret and Charles Huddleston
Jill Hughes
George and Mary Hurvey
Shel Izen
Lynette Janssen
Jim Jenkins
Troy Jenkins

Edward and Linda Jennings
Doug Jensen
Phillis and Ray Johnson
Paul Joyner
Alice Kahn
Shirley Keller
Florence and Leo Keopple
Ann Kerr
Thomas Kiehl
Jack and Norma Kinion
 (White River Red's Antiques)
Lori Kitchen
Jean Kocmond
Frank and Liz Kramer
Ruth Kulhanek
Lois Lehner
Sandy Levine
Gena Lightle (As Time Goes By)
Annette Littman
Juliana Lloyd
Mrs. M.J. Lucas
Jack and Norma Majewski
Grant and Carole Martin
Cathy McCulty
Jim Mederios
Margaret Merryman
Jane Millett
Ronna Miltmore
Mary Mims
John Moses
Donald and Lela Mutch
Larry and Bonnie Newlin
Bob Novak

Acknowledgments

Donna Obwald
Florence and Lyle Ohlendorf
Janet Parks
Judie Perez
Ron Perrick
Jill Peterson
Diane Petipas (Mood Indigo)
Stephen Ponder
Dave Prichard
  (Gray Barn Photography)
Steven Prickett
Charles and Pam Reed
Jim Rodgers
Mark Rumbolo
Frank Sargent
Linda Saridakis
Randy Sauder
Barbara Seimsen
Robert Sell, Jr.

Steve Sfakis
Terry Sfakis
Peter Shalit
Ronald Sidel
Rick and Joanne Simpson
Sam and Jennifer Skillern
Jean Stack
Dennis Stasiak
Tom and Toni Staugh
William Straus
Mike Sullivan (As Time Goes By)
Jan Sweet
Lois Szemko
Tom Taylor
Terry Telford
Les and Brenda Tesch (III)
Gregory Thompson
Lorna Thornton

Dan Tucker
Ernest Tucking
Kay & Joe Vahey
Bill Van Voorhies
Joan Vermette
Vance & Amy Vogeli
Lorraine Walker
Charles Walter
Carole Watkins
Clyde Watson
Harry Weitkemper
Joy Willems
Joel Wilson (China Specialties)
Rod Wilson
Ann Wise
Ronnie and Jean Woods
Michael and Carol Wowk
Catherine Yronwode

Here are bits of information we wanted to pass along to you, answers to some often-asked questions, and a tip or two you might find helpful.

If you're in the Newell/East Liverpool area, plan to stop off for a visit to the Homer Laughlin Pottery Company. Many of the morgue pieces are on display there, and tours are available. You'll be able to buy new Fiesta at the factory outlet store. (That number is 304-1300 extension 668.)

There are some very good collectors' organizations and tradepapers you will enjoy.

**The Fiesta Collector's
Quarterly Newsletter
PO Box 471
Valley City, OH 44280**

Sample copy on request and receipt of long SASE. For collectors of old and new Fiesta. Features regular updates of new colors and items added to new Fiesta line.

**The Fiesta Club of America
PO Box 15383
Loves Park, IL 61132-5383**

Membership fee, $20.00. Newsletter published four times a year. National conventions.

**Depression Glass Daze
Teri Steel, Editor/Publisher
Box 57
Otisville, MI 48463**

810-631-4593. The nation's marketplace for glass, china, and pottery.

**Homer Laughlin Collectors Club (HLCC)
PO Box 16174
Loves Park, IL 61132-6174**

Dues $20.00 per year, includes The Homer Laughlin Glaze, issued quarterly.

Many of you have asked where to buy new Fiesta. This listing is by no means complete:

Bloomingdale's Department Stores
Macy's Department Stores
Lazarus Department Stores

Roots Department Stores
Dayton's Department Stores
JC Penney's (catalog)

Speigel's (catalog)
House of 1776 (catalog)
Betty Crocker (premium catalog)

To remove cutlery marks from Fiesta, use a non-abrasive cleaner such as Soft Scrub or Semichrome. And yes, you may wash your Fiesta in the dishwasher; it is ovenproof, and the only color we've personally ever had a problem with putting in the microwave was red. Until next time...

Sharon and Bob

The Laughlin Pottery Story

The Laughlin Pottery was formed in 1871 on the River Road in East Liverpool, Ohio, the result of a partnership between Homer Laughlin and his brother, Shakespeare Laughlin. The pottery was equipped with two periodic kilns and was among the first in the country to produce whitewares. Sixty employees produced approximately five hundred dozen pieces of dinnerware per day. The superior quality of their pottery won for them the highest award at the Centennial Exposition in Philadelphia in 1876.

In 1879 Shakespeare Laughlin left the pottery; for the next ten years Homer Laughlin carried on the business alone. William Edwin Wells joined him in 1889; and at the end of 1896, the firm incorporated. Shortly thereafter, Laughlin sold his interests to Wells and a Pittsburgh group headed by Marcus Aaron.

Under the new management, Mr. Aaron became president, with Mr. Wells acting in the capacity of secretary-treasurer and general manager.

As their business grew and sales increased, the small River Road plant was abandoned, and the company moved its location to Laughlin Station, three miles east of East Liverpool. Two large new plants were constructed and a third purchased from another company. By 1903 all were ready for production. A fourth plant was built in 1906 at the Newell, West Virginia, site and began operations in 1907. In 1913 with business still increasing, Plant 5 was added.

The first revolutionary innovation in the pottery industry was the continuous tunnel kiln. In contrast to the old batch-type or periodic kilns which were inefficient from a standpoint of both fuel and time, the continuous tunnel kiln provided a giant step toward modern-day mass production. Plant 6, built in 1923, was equipped with this new type kiln and proved so successful that two more such plants were added — Plant 7 in 1927 and Plant 8 in 1929. The old kilns in Plants 4 and 5 were replaced in 1926 and 1934, respectively.

In 1929 the old East Liverpool factories were closed, leaving the entire operation at the Newell, West Virginia, site.

At the height of production, the company grew to a giant concern which employed 2,500 people, produced 30,000 dozen pieces of dinnerware per day, and utilized 1,500,000 square feet of production area. In contrast to the early wares painstakingly hand-fashioned in the traditional methods, the style of ware reflected the improved mass-production techniques which had of necessity been utilized in later years. The old-fashioned dipping tubs gave way to the use of high-speed conveyor belts and spray glazing, and mechanical jiggering machines replaced for the most part the older methods of man-powered molding machines.

In 1930 W.E. Wells retired from the business after more than forty years of brilliant leadership, having guided the development and expansion of the company from its humble beginning on the Ohio River to a position of unquestioned leadership in its field. He was succeeded by his son, Joseph Mahan Wells. Mr. Aaron became Chairman of the Board; his son, M.L. Aaron, succeeded him as President. Under their leadership, in addition to the successful wares already in production, many new developments made possible the production of a wide variety of utilitarian wares including the oven-to-table ware, OvenServe and Kitchen Kraft. Later, the creation of the beautiful glazes that have become almost synonymous with Homer Laughlin resulted in the production of the colored dinnerware lines which have captured the attention of many collectors today — Fiesta, Harlequin, and Riviera.

On January 1, 1960, Joseph M. Wells became chairman of the board, and his son, Joseph M. Wells, Jr., followed him in the capacity of executive vice-president.

Homer Laughlin continues today to be one of the principal dinnerware producers in the world.

The Story of Fiesta

In January of 1936, Homer Laughlin introduced a sensational new line of dinnerware at the Pottery and Glass Show in Pittsburgh. It was "Fiesta," and it instantly captured the imagination of the trade — a forecast of the success it was to achieve with housewives of America.

Fiesta was designed by Fredrick Rhead, an English Stoke-on-Trent potter whose work had for decades been regarded among the finest in the industry. His design was modeled by Arthur Kraft and Bill Bersford. The distinctive glazes were developed by Dr. A.V. Blenininger in association with H. W. Thiemecke.

This popularity was the result of much planning, market analysis, creative development, and a fundamentally sound and well-organized styling program. Rather than present to the everyday housewife a modernistic interpretation of a formal table service which might have been received with some reservation, HLC offered a more casual line with a well-planned series of accessories whose style was compatible with any decor and whose vivid colors could add bright spots of emphasis. Services of all types could be chosen and assembled at the whim of the housewife, and the simple style could be used compatibly with other wares already in her cabinets.

In an article by Fredrick Rhead, taken from the *Pottery and Glass Journal* for June, 1937, these steps toward Fiesta's development were noted: first, from oral descriptions and data concerning most generally used table articles, a chart of tentative sketches in various appealing colors was made. As the final ideas were formulated, they were modified and adjusted until development was completed. Secondly, the technical department made an intensive study of materials, composition, and firing temperatures. During this time, models and shapes were being studied. The result was to be a streamline shape, but not so obvious as to detract from the texture and color of the ware. It was to have no relief ornamentation and was to be pleasantly curving and convex, rather than concave and angular. Color was to be the chief decorative note; but to avoid being too severe, a concentric band of rings was to be added near the edges.

Since the early '30s, there had been a very definite trend in merchandising toward promoting "color." Automobiles, household appliances and furnishings, ladies' apparel — all took on vivid hues. The following is an excerpt from Rhead's article:

> The final selection of five colors was a more difficult job because we had developed hundreds of tone values and hues, and there were scores which were difficult to reject. Then there were textures ranging from dull mattes to highly reflecting surfaces. We tackled the texture problem first. (Incidentally, we had made fair-sized skeletons in each of the desirable glazes in order to be better able to arrive at the final selection.)
>
> We eliminated the dull mattes and the more highly reflecting glazes first, because in mass production practice, undue variation would result in unpleasant effects. The dull surfaces are not easy to clean, and the too highly reflecting surfaces show "curtains" or variations in thickness of application. We decided upon a semi-reflecting surface of about the texture of a billiard ball. The surface was soft and pleasant to the touch, and in average light there were no disturbing reflections to detract from the color and shape.
>
> We had one lead with regard to color. There seemed to be a trade preference for a brilliant orange-red. With this color as a keynote and with the knowledge that we were to have five colors, the problem resolved to one where the remainder would "tune in" or form appropriate contrasts.
>
> The obvious reaction to red, we thought, would be toward a fairly deep blue. We had blues ranging from pale turquoises to deep violet blues. The tests were made by arranging a table for four people; and, as the plate is an important item in the set, we placed four plates on various colored cloths and then arranged the different blues around the table. It seemed that the deeper blues reacted better than the lighter tones and blues which were slightly violet or purple. We also found that we had to do considerable switching before we could decide upon the right red. Some were too harsh and deep, others too yellow.

With the red and blue apparently settled, we decided that a green must be one of the five colors. We speedily discovered that the correct balance between the blue and the red was a green possessing a minimum of blue. We had to hit halfway between the red and the blue. We had some lovely subtle greens when they were not placed in juxtaposition with the other two colors, but they would not play in combination.

The next obvious color was yellow, and this had to be toned halfway between the red and the green. Only the most brilliant yellow we could make would talk in company with the other three.

The fifth color was the hardest nut to crack. Black was too heavy, although this may have been used if we could have had six or more colors. We had no browns, purples, or grays which would tune in. We eliminated all except two colors: a rich turquoise and a lovely color we called rose ebony. But there seemed to demand a quieting influence; so we tried an ivory vellum textured glaze which seemed to fit halfway between the yellow and the regular semi-vitreous wares and which cliqued when placed against any of the four colors selected. It took a little time to sell the ivory to our sales organization; but when they saw the table arrangements, they accepted the idea.

In the same publication a month earlier, Rhead had offered this evaluation of the popularity of the various colors with the public:

When this ware first appeared on the market, we attempted to estimate the preference for one color in comparison with the others. As you know, we make five colors . . . Because the red was the most expensive color, we thought this might affect the demand. And also, because green had previously been a most popular color, some guessed that this would outsell the others. However, to date, the first four colors are running neck and neck, with less than one percent difference between them. This is a remarkable result and amply bears out...that the "layman" prefers to mix his colors.

Company price lists have always been our main source of information. Over the years as more and more have been found, we have been able to pinpoint important production changes more accurately. Lists found as recently as this decade have clarified some misconceptions that resulted simply from not having them available for our original study. Our earliest is dated May 15, 1937; it lists fifty-four items. An article in the August 1936 issue of *China, Glass, and Lamps* reported new developments in the line since it had been introduced in January:

New items in the famous Fiesta line of solid-color dinnerware include egg cups; deep 8" plates; Tom and Jerry mugs; covered casseroles; covered mustards; covered marmalades; quart jugs; utility trays; flower vases in 8", 10", and 12" sizes; and bowl covers in 5", 6", 7", and 8" sizes.

By the process of elimination, then, in trying to determine the items original to the line, these must be subtracted from those on our May 1937 price list. A collector who has compiled the most complete assortment of company price lists that we are aware of tells us that the 10-oz. tumbler, the 6-cup (medium) teapot, and the 10½" compartment plate that are listed on our May '37 pamphlet were not yet listed on the Fall of 1936 issue which he has in his collection; so these would also have to be eliminated. These items remain, and until further information proves us wrong, we assume that they comprised the original assortment: coffeepot, regular; teapot, large; coffeepot, A.D.; carafe; ice pitcher; covered sugar bowl; creamer; bud vase; chop plate, 15"; chop plate, 13"; plate, 10"; plate, 9"; plate, 7"; plate, 6"; compartment plate, 12"; teacup and saucer; coffee cup and saucer, A.D.; footed salad bowl; nested bowls, 11½" to 5"; cream soup cup; covered onion soup; relish tray; compote, 12"; nappy, 9½"; nappy, 8½"; dessert, 6"; fruit, 5"; ashtray; sweets compote; bulb-type candle holders; tripod candle holders; and salt and pepper shakers.

Adding to the selling possibilities of Fiesta, in June 1936 the company offered their "Harmony" dinnerware sets. These combined their Nautilus line decorated with a colorful decal pattern, accented and augmented with the Fiesta color selected for that particular set. N-258 featured yellow Fiesta accenting Nautilus in white decorated with a harmonizing floral decal at the rim; N-259 used green Fiesta to complement a slender spray of pine cones. Red Fiesta, in N-260, was shown in company catalogs with Nautilus decorated with lines and leaves in an Art Deco motif (see Kitchen Kraft, OvenServe for matching kitchenware items); and blue (N-261) went well with white Nautilus with an off-center flower-filled basket decal. These sets were composed of sixty-seven pieces in all. Of the Nautilus shape there were 9" plates (8), 6" plates (8), teacups and saucers (8), 5½" fruits (8), a 10" baker, and a 9" nappy. Fiesta items included 10" plates (8), 7" plates (8), 6" plates (8), a 15" chop plate, a 12" compote, one pair of bulb-type candlesticks, a pair of salt and pepper shakers, and a creamer and sugar bowl. Retail price for such a set was around $20.00. This offered a complete service for eight and extra pieces that allowed for buffet and party service for as many more in the contrasting items.

For some time during the earlier years of production, beautifully accessorized "Fiesta Ensembles" were assembled — you will see a picture of a display ad showing such a set in the color plates. It contains 109 pieces, only forty of which are Fiesta: 9" plates (8), 6" plates (8), teacups and saucers (8), and 5" fruits (8). Accessories included a 24-pc. glassware set with enameled Mexican motifs. There were eight of each of the following: 10-oz., 8-oz., and 6-oz. tumblers; color-coordinated swizzle sticks; and glass ashtrays. A flatware service for eight with color-coordinated Catalin handles, a red Riviera serving bowl, a 15½" red Riviera platter, and a sugar and creamer in green Riviera completed the set. The flatware and glassware in these ensembles were manufactured by other companies and merely shipped to HLC to be distributed with the ensemble. Records fail to identify the company that may have manufactured these complementary accessories. Included in the packing carton was a promotional poster advertising this set for $14.95.

Originally all five colors sold at the same price; bud vases and salt and pepper shakers were priced in pairs. But on the May '37 price list, red items were higher than the other colors. For example, a red 12" flower vase was priced at $2.35; in the other colors it was only $1.85. A red onion soup was $1.00, 25¢ higher than the others. New to the assortment at that time were the three items mentioned earlier — the 6-cup (medium) teapot, the 10½" compartment plate, and the 10-oz. tumbler. Bud vases and salt and pepper shakers were priced singularly.

A few years ago a mid-1937 price list told us that the sixth color, turquoise, was added then and not in early '38 as we had previously reported. There is a 5" fruit on the May list; however, by mid-'37 the listing shows a 5½" and 4¾" fruit. Possibly the 5" and the 5½" are the same size fruit, with the so-called 5" listed actual size in mid-'37 due to the addition of the 4¾" size. (In comparing actual measurements to listed measurements, we have found variations of as much as ¾".) At this point, the first item had been discontinued; the 12" compartment plate was no longer available. The covered onion soup (evidently much more popular with today's collectors than it was then) was the second item to be dropped; by late that year it, too, was out of production. Two new items were added in the Fall of 1937, the sauce boat and the 11½" low fruit bowl. The assortment remained the same until the following July when the disk water jug and the 12" oval platter made their first appearance on company listings. No further changes were made until October 1939, when the stick-handled creamer was replaced by the creamer with the ring handle.

From 1939 through 1943, the company was involved in a promotional campaign designed to stimulate sales. This involved several special items, each of which was offered for sale at $1.00. An ad from the February 1940 *China, Glass, and Lamps* magazine provides us with the information concerning the campaign.

> ...dollar retailers in Fiesta ware include covered French casserole; 4-pc. refrigerator set; sugar, creamer, and tray set; salad bowl with fork and spoon; casserole with pie plate; chop plate with detachable metal holder; and jumbo coffee cups and saucers in blue, pink, and yellow.

But it also presents us with a puzzling question: what were the jumbo coffee cups and saucers? Sit 'n Sips perhaps? (See Miscellaneous.) The colors mentioned, though dark blue and yellow were in production in 1940, sound pastel with the inclusion of pink. Anyone have an answer? We don't!

Another item featured in the selling campaign is described in this message from HLC to their distributors:

> JUICE SET IN FIESTA . . . To help increase your sales! Homer Laughlin is offering an unusual value in the famous Fiesta ware . . . a colorful, 7-piece Juice Set, calculated to fill a real need in the summer refreshment field. The set consists of a 30-oz. disk jug in lovely Fiesta yellow, and six 5 oz. tumblers, one each in Fiesta blue, turquoise, red, green, yellow, and ivory. Sets come packed one to a carton, and at the one dollar minimum retail price are sure to create an upward surge in your sales curve. Dealers who take advantage of this Juice Set in Fiesta will find it a potent weapon in increasing sales of other Fiesta items. At a nominal price, customers who have not yet become acquainted with Fiesta can own some of the ware which has made pottery history during the past few years. The result? They'll want to own more!

Although the other promotional items are relatively scarce, the yellow juice pitcher is very easily found. This flyer is the only mention of it being for sale during this period; neither it nor the juice tumblers were ever included on Fiesta price lists. A few pitchers have been found in red, and only recently has evidence surfaced to explain that at least some of them were special ordered by the Reliable Tea Company, who offered the juice sets (red pitcher and six assorted juice tumblers) as premiums to their customers during the decade of the 1940s. In 1952 the promotion was repeated – the juice pitcher in gray, the tumblers in dark green, chartreuse, and Harlequin yellow. Either this issue was not extensively promoted or proved to be a poor seller, judging from their scarcity in these colors. Juice tumblers in rose are not at all rare, yet in this color they were not mentioned in any of these promotions. A factory spokesman explained this to us: while rose was not a standard Fiesta color until the '50s, it had been developed and was in use with the Harlequin line during the '40s. Since it was available in the dipping department, it was used to add extra color contrast to the juice set.

The French casserole, individual sugar and creamer on the figure-8 tray, and the 9½" salad bowl were also never listed except in this promotion. Each is standard in a specific color; on rare occurrences when they are found in non-standard glazes, their values soar! (See pricing information in the back of the book.) French casseroles were all to have been yellow; however, two dark blue bases and one complete casserole have been reported, and a lid and base have been found in light green. Before the fifth edition was published, we received a letter telling us that an ivory one existed. Just before this edition went to press, its current owners wrote to verify its existence. Yellow was also standard for the 9½" salad bowl, but a very few have surfaced in dark blue, red, ivory, and light green. The individual sugars and creamers were to be yellow, the trays dark blue. One sugar and at least two creamers have been found in turquoise, red creamers have been reported though they are very rare, and just recently a reliable, advanced collector assures us that his cobalt creamer is old Fiesta, not one from the new line. He explains that the cobalt is the lighter "old" shade and that the piece is of the thinner gauge associated with the original. Trays in yellow or turquoise have been found, but these, too, are very rare.

One of the most exciting discoveries of this decade is the three-piece Fiesta Kitchenware Set referred to in the list of $1.00 promotions as "casserole with pie plate." See the Fiesta color plates for a look at this exciting set photographed with its original carton. We're sure it's authentic, since it was originally found in the unopened carton. The casserole is the one that has been a mystery for years. Though we suspected it to be a Homer Laughlin product years ago, the company rep didn't recall that they had ever produced such a casserole. However, before he retired, he sent us a photocopy of a promotional sheet verifying the casserole to be theirs. (See Plate 9.)

Other items that have never been included on any known price list are the syrup pitcher and the very rare flat 10" cake plate. It was only recently that we found a list containing the four smaller sizes of the nested bowl lids that were mentioned in Rhead's article. A butter dish was never listed with Fiesta, but the consensus of opinion after so many years of collecting is that the Jade/Riviera butter dish (see Plate 359 for more information) was dipped to go with the Fiesta line as well, since it may be found in cobalt and ivory, both standard colors in only one of HLC's lines, Fiesta.

More changes occurred in the Fall of 1942. Items discontinued at that time included the tripod candle holders, the A.D. coffeepot, and both the 10" and 12" flower vases.

In 1943 our government assumed control of uranium oxide, an important element used in the manufacture of the Fiesta red glaze. As a result, it was dropped from production — "Fiesta red went to war." Perhaps the fact that Fiesta red had been listed separately and priced proportionately higher than the other colors was due to the higher cost of raw material plus the fact that the red items required strict control during firing; losses that did occur had to be absorbed in the final costs.

The color assortment in 1944 included turquoise, green, blue, yellow, and ivory. The nested bowls no longer were listed. The rate of price increases over the seven years Fiesta had been on the market is hard for us to imagine: ashtrays were still only 15¢, egg cups were up to 35¢ from 30¢, relish trays were up only 15¢ to $1.80 complete.

Although the colors are listed the same on the 1946 price list, the following pieces were discontinued: bud vase, bulb-type candle holders, carafe, 12" compote, sweets compote, 8" vase, 11½" fruit bowl, ice pitcher, marmalade and mustard, 9½" nappy, relish tray, footed salad bowl, large teapot, 10-oz. tumbler, and utility tray.

A price list from November 5, 1950, helps us pinpoint the time of the radical color change that had taken place by October of 1951. Though the 1950 price list still offered the original colors, by fall of 1951 light green, dark blue, and old ivory had been retired; their replacements were forest green, rose, chartreuse, and gray. Turquoise and yellow continued to be produced. These four new colors have been dubbed "'50s colors," since they and the listed assortment remained in production without change until the end of the decade.

Prices listed in 1956, twenty years after Fiesta was introduced, were higher, of course; but still the increase is so slight as to be quite noteworthy to us in the '90s. Ashtrays sold for 40¢, teacups that were 25¢ were up to 65¢. Dinner plates had little more than doubled at 90¢, and coffeepots sold for $2.65. They, too, had about doubled in price.

The big news in 1959 was, of course, the fact that Fiesta red was reinstated. It was welcomed back with much ado! The Atomic Energy Commission licensed the Homer Laughlin China Company to again buy the depleted uranium oxide, and Fiesta red returned to the market in March of 1959.

In addition to red, turquoise, and yellow, a new color — medium green — was offered. Rose, gray, chartreuse, and dark green were discontinued; and the following items were no longer available: 15" chop plate, A.D. coffee cup and saucer, regular coffeepot, 10½" compartment plate, cream soup cup, egg cup, 4¾" fruit bowl, and the 2 pt. jug. A new item made an appearance — the individual salad bowl.

By 1961 the 6" dessert bowl was no longer listed. Aside from that change, the line and the color assortment remained the same. Though retail prices had risen in 1965; by 1968 some items stayed the same while others actually dropped slightly.

In the latter months of 1969 in an effort to meet the needs of the modern housewife and to present a product that was better designed to be in keeping with modern day decor, Fiesta was restyled. Only one of the original colors, Fiesta red — always the favorite — continued in production (see chapter on Fiesta Ironstone).

The big news of 1986 was the exciting new line of Fiesta ware that was introduced in the Spring. How better to celebrate its fiftieth birthday! We'll tell you all about it in one of the following chapters.

The Radioactive Red

Exactly when the first rumors began circulating, hinting that the red Fiesta could be "hazardous" to your health, is uncertain. In most probability, it was around the time that Fiesta red was reintroduced after the war and was no doubt due to the publicity given to uranium and radioactivity during the war years. Clearly another case where "a little learning can be a dangerous thing."

In any case, this worry must have remained to trouble the minds of some people for several years. Even today the subject comes up occasionally and remains a little controversial, though most folks in this troubled age of acid rains, high unemployment, cholesterol-free diets, and constant reminders that "cigarettes are hazardous to your health" don't really seem too upset by it anymore.

The following letter appeared in the *Palm Beach Post Times* in February 1963. It was written tongue-in-cheek by a man who had evidently reached the limit of his patience. HLC sent it to us from their files; it has to be a classic.

> Editor:
>   After reading about the radioactive dishes in your paper, I am greatly concerned that I may be in danger, as I had a plate with a design in burnt orange, or maybe it was lemon.
>   This plate was left to me by my great-grandmother, and I noticed that whenever she ate anything from it, her ears would light up; so we all had to wear dark glasses when dining at her house.
>   I first became suspicious of this dish when putting out food for my dog on it I noticed the dog's nose became as red as Rudolph's; and one day a sea gull fed from it, and all his feathers fell off; then one night when the weather was raw I placed it at the foot of my bed, and my toenails turned black.
>   Using it as a pot cover while cooking eel stew, the pot cracked; and reading the letters in your paper last week have concluded I am not the only person having a cracked pot in the house; so perhaps some of your other readers used a plate for a cover.
>   I finally threw this plate overboard at a turn in the channel, now a buoy is no longer needed there, as bubbles and steam mark this shoal.
>   Will you please ask your Doctor or someone if they think this plate is radioactive, and if so am I in any danger, and if so from what?
>
> (Name Withheld)

Several years ago we were allowed the opportunity to search through old company literature in the event that some bit of pertinent information had escaped our notice. It was obvious from letters contained in these files that HLC had always been harassed with letters from people concerned with the uranium content of the Fiesta red glaze. Their replies were polite, accommodating, and enlightening. Here in part is one of their letters:

> Before 1943 the colorant (14% by weight of the glaze covering the ware) is uranium oxide (U-308), with the uranium content being made up of about 0.7% U-235 and the remainder U-238. Between 1943 and 1959 under license by AEC, we have again been producing a red glazed dinnerware. However the colorant now used is depleted technical grade U-308 with the uranium content being made up of about 0.2% U-235 and the remainder U-238.

Studies were conducted for us by Dr. Paul L. Ziemer and Dr. Geraldine Deputy (who is herself an avid Fiesta collector) in the Bionuclionics Department of Purdue University. The penetrating radiation from the uranium oxide used in the manufacturing of the glaze for the red Fiesta ware was measured with a standard laboratory Geiger Counter. All measurements are tabularized in units of milliroentgens per hour (mR/hr).

Item	Surface Contract	4" Above Surface	Along Rim
13" Chop Plate	0.8	0.35	0.1
9" Plate	0.5	1.5	0.07
Fruit Bowl	1.5	0.5	0.1
Relish Tray Wedge	0.8	0.2	0.02
Cup	1.3	0.2	0.03

In order to compare the above values to familiar quantities of radiation, we calculated the exposure of a person holding a 13" chop plate strapped to his chest for twenty-four hours. This gives twenty milliroentgens per day. Safe levels for humans working with radiation is one hundred milliroentgens per week for a five-day week or twenty milliroentgens per day as background radiation.

Some other measurements of interest for comparison purposes are:

Item	Radiation
Radium Dial on a Watch	20mR/hr
Chest X-Ray	44 mR per film
Dental X-Ray	910 mR per film
Fatal Dose	400,000 mR over whole body

So you see — unless you've noticed your grandmother's nose glowing — we're all quite safe!

One other small worry to put to rest (some have mentioned it): there is no danger from the fired-on glazes, which are safe as opposed to a shellac-type color which could mix with acid from certain foods and result in lead poisoning.

Back in May of 1977 on an eastern television station, an announcement was made concerning the pros and cons of the safety of colored-glazed dinnerware. Fiesta was mentioned by name. We contacted the Department of Health, Education and Welfare, FDA, in Chicago, Illinois. This in part is their position, and it is supported by HLC:

> The presence of lead, cadmium, and other toxic metal in glaze or decal is not in itself a hazard. It becomes a problem only when a glaze or decal that has not been properly formulated, applied, or fired, contains dangerous metals which can be released by high-acid foods such as fruit juices, some soft drinks, wines, cider, vinegar, and vinegar-containing foods, sauerkraut, and tomato products.

HLC passed the rigorous federal tests with flying colors! In fact, the only examples of earthenware posing a threat to consumers were imported, and hobbyists were warned to use extreme caution in glazing hand-thrown ceramics.

The FDA report continues:

> Be on the safe side by not storing foods or beverages in such containers for prolonged periods of time, such as overnight. Daily use of the dinnerware for serving food does not pose a hazard. If the glaze or decal is properly formulated, properly applied, and properly fired, there is no hazard.

...R.I.P.

~Identification of Trademark, Design, and Color~

Fiesta's original design, colors, and name are the registered property of the Homer Laughlin China Company. Patent No. 390-298 was filed on March 20, 1937, having been used by them since November 11, 1935. With only a few exceptions, their distinctive trademark appears on every piece. These four seem to be the most common.

The indented trademark was the result of in-mold casting; the ink mark was put on with a hand stamp after the color was applied and before the final glaze was fired.

As many other manufacturers were following the trend to brightly colored dinnerware, the wide success and popularity of Fiesta resulted in its being closely copied and produced at one time by another company. Homer Laughlin quickly brought suit against their competitor and forced the imitation ware to be discontinued. To assure buyers they could buy with complete confidence, the word "Genuine" was added to the hand stamp sometime before 1940. Genuine Fiesta was the exclusive product of Homer Laughlin.

There are some items in the Fiesta line which were never meant to be marked — juice tumblers, demitasse cups, salt and pepper shakers, teacups, and some of the Kitchen Kraft line. But a few teacups, demitasse cups, and salt and pepper shakers have been found with the ink stamp. Sweets compotes, ashtrays, and onion soups may or may not be marked. Never pass up a "goodie" such as these simply because they are unmarked! As you become more aware of design and color, these pieces will be easily recognized as Fiesta.

Fiesta's design is very simple and therefore very versatile. The pattern consists of a band of concentric rings graduating in width, with those nearer the rim being more widely spaced. The rings are repeated in the center motif on such pieces as plates, nappies, platters, desserts, etc. Handles are applied with slight ornamentation at the base. Vases and tripod candle holders, though designed without the rings, are skillfully modeled with simple lines, geometric forms, and stepped devices that instantly relate to the Art Deco mood of Fiesta's clean uncluttered shapes. Flat pieces and bowls are round or oval; hollow ware pieces are globular, and many are styled with a short pedestal base decorated with the band of rings.

But, of course, it's Fiesta's vivid colors that first capture your attention. The wide array of color provides endless possibilities for matching color schemes and decor. And if you find you love all eleven, you'll surely enjoy collecting a place setting in every color — Fiesta red, yellow, rose, old ivory, gray, dark blue, turquoise, forest green, light green, medium green, and chartreuse.

Dating Codes and English Measurements

Many HLC lines often carry a backstamp containing a series of letters and numbers. The company has provided this information to help you in deciphering these codes:

In 1900 the trademark featured a single numeral identifying the month, a second single numeral identifying the year, and a numeral 1, 2, or 3 designating the point of manufacture as East Liverpool, Ohio.

In the period 1910–20, the first figure indicated the month of the year, the next two numbers indicated the year, and the third figure designated the plant. No. 4 was "N," No. 5 was "N5," and the East End plant was "L."

A change was made for the period of 1921–1930. The first letter was used to indicate the month of the year such as "A" for January, "B" for February, "C" for March. The next single digit number was used to indicate the year, and the last figure designated the plant.

For the period 1931– 40, the month was expressed as a letter; but the year was indicated with two digits. Plant No. 4 was "N," No. 5 was "R," No. 6 and 7 were "C" and No. 8 was listed as "P." During this period, E-44R5 would indicate May of 1944 and manufactured by Plant No. 5. The current trademark has been in use for approximately seventy years, and the numbers are the only indication of the specific years that items were produced.

Collectors have long been puzzled over the origin and meaning of such terms as oval "baker" and "36s bowl" — not to mention the insistent listings of 4" plates, when it has become very apparent that 4" plates do not exist! We asked our contact at HLC for an explanation. He told us that each size bowl was assigned a number. Smaller numbers indicated larger bowls, and vice versa. The word "baker" as used to describe a serving bowl was an English potting term. It was also the English who established the unfortunate system of measurements based on some rather obscure logic by which a 6" plate should be listed as 4". The 7" "nappies" (also an English term) actually measure 8¾"; 4" fruits are usually 5½"; and 6", 7", and 8" plates are in reality 7", 9", and 10".

This practice continued through the '50s (though more in connection with other HLC lines than Fiesta) until it became so utterly confusing to everyone involved that actual measurements were thankfully adopted. However, these may vary as much as ¾" from measurements listed on company brochures. For instance, 9" and 10" plates actually measure 9½" and 10½", and the 13" and 15" chop plates are 12¼" and 14¼".

The small incised letters and/or numbers sometimes found on the bottom of hollow ware pieces were used to identify a pieceworker — perhaps a molder or a trimmer — and were intended for quality control purposes. More likely to appear on Harlequin, these are sometimes seen on Fiesta as well.

Fredrick Hurten Rhead

The Rhead family was prominent among the finest ceramists of nineteenth-century England. Fredrick Hurten Rhead came from a long line of English Stoke-on-Trent potters and must without doubt be considered one of the most productive artisans in the history of the industry. At the age of 19, he was named Art Director at the Wardel Pottery. After leaving his home in Staffordshire in 1902, he worked at the Vance/Avon Faience Co. in Tiltonville, Ohio, for a term of about six months before moving on to the Weller Pottery in Zanesville, Ohio. By 1904 he was awarded the position of Art Director at the nearby Roseville Pottery. The many lines of artware he produced for these companies earned him widespread recognition. Inspired by nature and influenced by both Art Nouveau and the Arts and Crafts Movement, he became well known for dramatic sgraffito work, which he executed in intricate detail. An element he often favored was a stylized tree, variations of which he used frequently throughout his career. In later years, he designed a set of nested mixing bowls for Homer Laughlin; they were decorated with embossed trees reminiscent of his earlier work.

Leaving Roseville in 1908, he went to the William Jervis Pottery on Long Island. In 1909 he accepted the post of Instructor in Pottery at the University City Pottery in St. Louis. From 1911 to 1913 he was associated with the Arequipa Pottery in Fairfax, California. There, with the assistance of his wife, Agnes, he taught ceramics to patients at the Arequipa Sanatorium. Leaving Arequipa, he organized the Pottery of the Camarata in Santa Barbara, later to be incorporated as The Rhead Pottery. Never a confident thrower, Rhead involved himself fully with developing new glazes. One of his finest achievements was Mirror Black, a recreation of the sixteenth-century black-glazed pottery of the Orient, which earned him a Gold Medal at the 1915 San Diego Exposition.

In December of 1916, Rhead published *The Potter*, a monthly magazine dealing with the progress of the industry. The editor of the historical department was Edwin A. Barber, whose death was reported in the third issue (February, 1917). With that, the paper was abandoned.

Freed of the pressures he had felt at the commercial potteries in Ohio, Rhead utilized this time to develop his creative capabilities to their fullest, but as a business man he was unable to keep his pottery afloat. He encountered financial difficulties, and his pottery failed. Returning to Zanesville in 1917, he joined the American Encaustic Tiling Company. Loiz Whitcomb, a fellow artisan from his California pottery (with whom he had fallen in love after his first marriage was annulled), came back to the Midwest to join him; they soon married. Rhead served at AE Tile as Director of Research. In 1927 he moved to the Homer Laughlin Company where he designed his famous dinnerware line, Fiesta. He remained there until his death in 1942. No other ceramic artist made more of an impact on this country's pottery industry.

From the early days of his career to the last, Rhead's work evolved effortlessly, leaving behind a legacy still enjoyed by thousands today.

Shown at right are examples of only two of the lines Rhead developed for Roseville and Weller — Della Robbia on the right, and Weller Rhead Faience on the left.

Plate 1

Footed Salad Bowl (left).

These not only hold salad for more people than you'd probably care to entertain but make great punch bowls as well. They're not too easily found. They were made from the time Fiesta was introduced until 1946 in only the first six colors (this prize is Fiesta red, of course) with ivory and yellow reported to be the hardest to find. They're listed as being 12" in diameter but are actually only 11¼".

Fruit Bowl (right).

These are hard to find, especially in red. They were made from 1937 until sometime between 1944 and 1946 in the six original colors. They're shallow, only 3" deep and 11¾" in diameter.

Plate 2

Ashtray.

Shown here in dark green, these were made from 1936 until the Fiesta Ironstone line was discontinued in 1973, and they can be found in all of the old colors plus Turf Green and Antique Gold. They are 5½" in diameter.

Plate 1

Plate 2

Plate 3

Covered Onion Soup Bowl (left foreground).

Imagine a lifestyle that required a soup bowl with a lid! They're very scarce today, so even back in the more formal '30s, they probably were never good sellers. They can be found in ivory, red, light green (shown), dark blue, turquoise and yellow. (See an example of each in Plate 5.) Since they were discontinued by Fall of 1937, only a few weeks after turquoise was added to the color assortment (mid-'37), they're very scarce in that color. A few years ago, a collector reported a set of eight, all in turquoise — the find of a lifetime! Another unusual set of eight has been found in ivory with a red stripe. (For an example, see Plate 70 in the section on Striped Fiesta.)

Dessert Bowl (upper left).

This is another item that was in the original line. Shown here in dark blue, it was produced until 1961 in all colors, but it's scarce in medium green. They're 6" in diameter.

Individual Salad Bowl (center back).

A later addition, these were not produced until 1959 and were, of course, only made in the colors of that period — red, turquoise, yellow, and medium green. They're easier to find in red and medium green; nevertheless expect to pay a premium for medium green, regarded by collectors as Fiesta's most desirable color. Occasionally you may find one with no rings in the bottom, probably produced toward the transition into Fiesta Ironstone when such modifications were finalized. Collectors are also reporting bowls in all four colors as well as the brighter Harlequin yellow with no inside rings at all.

Fruit Bowl, 5½" (upper right).

Probably the bowl listed as 5" in the original assortment, this item was made until the restyling in 1969 and is available in all eleven colors (yellow is shown).

Fruit Bowl, 4¾" (right foreground).

This was probably the bowl that was added to the assortment in mid-'37. We have price lists that are dated 1956 and 1959; they show it as still available in 1956, but it does not appear on the 1959 price list when medium green was introduced, and only a few have been found in that color. It's rather scarce in red as well; here you see it in the rose of the '50s assortment.

Plate 4

Cream Soup Bowl.

These were part of the original line and continued to be made until sometime in 1959. They're found in all colors but are very rare in medium green, the newcomer to the color assortment that year.

Plate 3

Plate 4

Plate 5
This is a rare view of the covered onion soup bowls, one in each color of their production. The very rare turquoise example in the front row is especially noteworthy.

Plate 5

Plate 6

Plate 6

This photo is for all of you who are nested bowl collectors. We wanted to show you just how fantastic the completed collection looks.

Plate 7

Mixing Bowls.

Stacked together, a set weighs almost twenty pounds. These bowls were made in only the original six colors, since they were in production from 1936 until around 1943. Each bowl is numbered in sequence on the bottom, #1 being the smallest. There are seven sizes, ranging from 5" to 11½". We were recently sent a copy of a full-page ad dated December 1938, from which we learned that as a promotion during the Christmas season that year (and for only $2.50), you could purchase a "Rainbow Mixing Bowl Set" — a four-piece assortment that contained a 7" yellow bowl, a 8" green one, a 9" one in dark blue and a 10" bowl in red. Collectors tell us the #7 (11½") bowl is difficult to find, perhaps because it wasn't included in this promotion, perhaps simply because fewer sold, since its size likely made it unwieldy to use. The #1 (5") bowl is also scarce, and that may also be contributed to its size. It might have been just right for storing leftovers, but as a mixing bowl, it's small! The only bowl lids ever officially offered on a company price list were the four smaller sizes — 5", 6", 7", and 8". Although the list we refer to is undated, we can place it after August 1936 (our price list bearing that date makes no mention of them) and before 1937 (because turquoise was not yet being offered on the list in question).

Plate 7

Plate 8

Bowl Lids.

They're extremely rare in any size! The #5 nested bowl lid remained undiscovered until just before our 1994 update; since then, at least three #6s have finally been unearthed, including the one in this fantastic, pristine all-red set! Is there a #7? According to old HLC records, there may just be!

Plate 9

Promotional Casserole and Pie Plate.

For many years collectors suspected that these casseroles had been made by Homer Laughlin, since they kept turning up in colors identical to several of HLC's standard glazes. Most of them are red, turquoise, yellow, light green, and mauve blue, though cobalt, Harlequin yellow, maroon, and spruce green have also been found. When we inquired, company representatives denied they ever produced them, and so for years we had no choice but to exclude them from the Fiesta lineup. But a few years ago, evidence surfaced to contradict that statement. (In their defense, few plant records were kept, and as we all know, memories tend to fail over so many years.) To begin with, the company themselves discovered an old order sheet showing their "#600 Gift Assortment of Colored Ware" — and there it was, our mystery casserole! Then the set in our photograph was found, still sealed in its original unopened carton which is stamped Fiesta on the side not shown. So, though no examples have ever been reported with the HLC mark, we feel sure that this is the "casserole with pie plate" offered in the promotional campaign of 1939–1942 for the price of only $1.00 per set. (For more information on this campaign, see pages 10-11.) The casserole is 3" deep and measures 8" in diameter. The Fiesta Kitchen Kraft pie plate is 9¾" (the smaller of the two shown later in the Fiesta Kitchen Kraft section).

Plate 8

Plate 10
Here is the metal holder that was shown on the order sheet we mentioned in the description for Plate 9. Artist renderings of the other two included in the "#600 Assortment" are shown in the chapter entitled "Go-Alongs," where you'll see several others as well. Collectors report finding this casserole in holders that vary slightly from the one we show here.

Plate 11
Nappy, 9½" (left).
   This bowl was part of the original assortment and was still listed on our 1944 price list, but by Fall of 1946 it was no longer available.
Nappy, 8½" (center).
   Here shown in medium green, these bowls were made from 1936 until the line was restyled in '69, so it comes in all eleven colors.
Unlisted Salad Bowl (right).
   Although this salad bowl (3¾" deep by 9½" in diameter) was never listed on the price pamphlets, a trade paper from 1940 reported on the Homer Laughlin sales campaign that offered this bowl accompanied by the Kitchen Kraft spoon and fork for only $1.00 — another of the "promotionals." The ad copy indicated that these bowls were offered in only yellow. They're very scarce even in that color, but a rare few have been reported in ivory, red, light green, and dark blue (see Plate 15).

Plate 10

Plate 9

Plate 11

Plate 12

French Casserole.

Another of the eight special promotional items offered by HLC from 1939 to '42, the French casserole is a relatively scarce item. Virtually all are yellow, though two bases and two complete units have been reported in dark blue, and a lid and base have been found in light green; just as we were nearing completion on this update, one was reported in ivory. The lid differs significantly enough from the one on the casserole in the next plate that you'll easily be able to tell which lid you have, should you find a spare. The French casserole lid measures 9" in diameter compared to 8" for the regular casserole lid, and the finial is ⅞" across the top compared to 1¼".

Plate 13

Casserole.

Considering that production of the "covered casserole" (as it was always listed) was continuous from 1936, they're not especially easy to find. This one is shown in dark green, which along with the other colors of the '50s (rose, gray, and chartreuse) is very desirable, but it goes without saying that a medium green example would top the list!

Plate 12

Plate 13

Plate 14

Plate 14

Tricolator Bowl.

This is simply the casserole bottom without the standard applied foot. It's another piece the company denied making, but collectors just don't buy it. It's marked Tricolator, a company that specialized in combining a piece such as this one with a warmer base, a metal frame, etc. It was common practice for a pottery company to make items such as this to fill a special order — not just for Tricolator, but for similar companies as well. You can also find coffeepots that were made for Tricolator by Hall, some of which bear the marks of both companies. These bowls have been reported in ivory, yellow, red, turquoise, green and cobalt. When found, they're normally open, though one collector tells us his was bought at an estate sale topped with the standard Fiesta casserole lid.

Plate 15

This is a very rare example of the unlisted salad bowl, shown here in dark blue. It's rare in ivory and red as well. Let's get a count! Do you have one in these colors?

Plate 16

The tripod candle holders in this photograph are a one-of-a-kind pair glazed in a beautiful aubergine that might be a match to the dark "red grape" experimental plate we saw in the morgue. It's been many years since our morgue trip, and colors are very difficult to remember accurately. Or could this and the color of the morgue plate as well be Rhead's "rose ebony?" (Rose Ebony is mentioned on page 9.) See Plate 18 for more information.

Plate 17

Bulb Candle Holders.

Both these and the tripod candle holders were part of the original line; this style was discontinued sometime between 1944 and late 1946. They were made in the six early colors and are relatively easy to find.

Plate 15

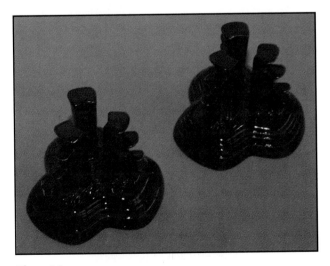

Plate 16

Plate 17

Plate 18

Tripod Candle Holders.

  These are regarded as very desirable additions to any collection. They've always been scarce and are even more so today. They were made in only the first six colors, since they were discontinued around 1942 or '43.

Plate 19

Carafe.

  The carafe was part of the original line but was no longer listed by 1946. The stopper has a cork seal, and its wonderful Deco lines make it a favorite among collectors. It was a turquoise carafe that caused us to become collectors. We bought it for a friend who, knowing our passion for flea markets, asked us to pick up Fiesta for her to add to the set she'd received for her wedding. This was the only piece we ever gave her, and we really hated to part with it. These were made in the first six colors only, with red and ivory being the most difficult to find. The company lists its capacity as three pints.

Plate 20

Coffeepot, Teacups and Saucers.

  The coffeepot can be found in all of Fiesta's colors except medium green. It was in the original line but was not made after mid-1956. Of course, teacups are always in demand. You'll find some interesting variations among teacups; these are discussed in more detail in Plate 24. Though cups are seldom marked, a rare few have been reported bearing the HLC ink stamp, sometimes in gold.

Plate 21

  This photo is a real attention-grabber! Unless you're one of those collectors who has to have every piece in every color (or personally know someone who is), here are more coffeepots than you've probably ever seen in one group before or ever will again — one in each of the ten colors in which they were made. (Notice the absence of medium green.)

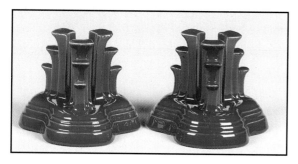

Plate 18

Plate 19

Plate 20

Photo by Richard Wright

Plate 21

Photo by Richard Wright

Plate 22

Demitasse Pot, Demitasse Cups and Saucers.

If you've never been sure of the meaning of the terms demitasse and "AD," they simply refer to small cups of strong black coffee meant to be slowly sipped and lingered over after a lovely dinner. Designed to serve after-dinner coffee with elegance and flair, demitasse pots and cups were included in the original line. The pot was discontinued before 1944; you'll find it in the six original colors only with turquoise examples being very rare. The cups and saucers supposedly were made in just ten colors — no medium green, since they were discontinued in '56, three years before that color was introduced — but four sets in medium green were just discovered. How exciting! Of the ten standard colors, the '50s colors are hardest to find and sell at a premium. A collector once reported finding one in a brick-red glaze.

Plate 23

This breathtaking lineup contains an example of all six colors of the demitasse pot. Note the vent hole showing in the lid of the yellow example. These holes were put in by hand and evidently most of the time and as a general rule regarded as a dispensable option.

Plate 24

There are three distinct styles of teacups — those with the inside rings (right) are the oldest. They also have a hand-turned foot. Only a few have been found in medium green which would seem to indicate that it was sometime around 1959 when the inside rings disappeared and the foot became part of the casting, no longer requiring expensive hand trimming. The teacup on the left represents the second style. Note that the third style (center back), though produced in the color assortment available through the '60s, has the "C" handle of Fiesta Ironstone — evidently manufactured near the time of the restyling. It's very rare to find a marked cup. (If your cup has a molded-in mark, it's new.)

Plate 22

Plate 23

Plate 24

Plate 25

Tom and Jerry Mug.

These are sometimes referred to as coffee mugs; they were reported in Rhead's article (mid-'36) as being new to the line and continued in production until the end. They were made in all eleven colors, though ivory examples are scarce. This one is dark blue and the photograph shows the trademark ring handle to perfection. You'll find some variation in the thickness of the walls as well as the height.

Plate 26

Marmalade and Mustard Jars.

Marmalades (the yellow one) and mustards (ours is red) were two of the items mentioned in Rhead's August 1936 magazine article quoted in the chapter entitled "The Story of Fiesta." He wrote that these were new to the line at that time. They were discontinued between 1944 and 1946, so they're found in the first six colors only. A collector reports finding a cobalt mustard with the gold ink stamp.

Plate 27

Sweets Comport.

We found that the sweets comports, part of the original assortment, were discontinued between 1944 and 1946, so they're available only in the six early colors. They are 3½" tall, and only about one out of four examples is marked with the ink stamp.

Plate 25

Plate 26

Plate 27

Plate 28

Comport.

These were made from 1936 until sometime between 1944 and '46. They're 12" in diameter and can be found in only the six original colors.

Plate 29

Egg Cup.

These were not part of the original line; they were added in mid-'36. They were discontinued between January and September of 1956 and are available in ten colors (no medium green). Collectors report that chartreuse and gray are the hardest to find.

Plate 30

Creamer and Sugar Bowl, Individual; Figure-8 Tray.

This set is from the 1939-'43 sales campaign. Nearly all sets are found with the sugar and creamer in yellow on a cobalt tray; however, occasionally you'll find a red creamer and once in awhile a turquoise or yellow tray. Though no more than two or three have been reported, creamers have been found in turquoise, and one turquoise sugar bowl is known to exist. These reports were prior to 1986. After the new line was introduced, a cobalt creamer was found by an advanced collector with many years' experience who is confident that it is old, and it has been verified as old by others who have seen it as well.

Plate 28

Plate 30

Plate 29

Plate 31

Creamer and Sugar Bowl.

Shown here in red, the creamer (which collectors call the "regular" creamer) replaced the original stick-handled version in the Fall of 1939 and continued in production until restyled for the Ironstone line. The sugar bowl remained basically the same from '36 on, though the bases of earlier creamers and sugar bowls are flared out as compared to those made in the late '40s in the original colors and those in the '50s colors, when a slight change in the molds resulted in a base with a rather stubby appearance.

Stick-Handled Creamer.

These were made from 1936 until late 1939 when they were replaced by the ring-handled style described above. They come in the six early colors and are hardest to find in turquoise (as shown).

Plate 32

A sales promotion offered in 1952 is represented here — a gray pitcher along with a pair of tumblers in each of these colors: dark green, Harlequin yellow, and chartreuse. These are very hard to find. One collector's theory, and it may well be fact, is that this set was dipped to go with Rhythm. The dates coincide, and the fact that only recently a collector sent us a photo of a juice tumbler in burgundy (maroon), the fourth Rhythm color, certainly seems to confirm this theory. The Rhythm theory was based on the premise that since Jubilee had been promoted with a Fiesta juice set and mixing bowls dipped to match the line, and we already knew there were Rhythm/Fiesta bowl sets, it made perfect sense that a juice set might also have been part of a Rhythm promotion.

Plate 33

This juice set was glazed in the Jubilee colors as part of a promotion to stimulate its sales. The gray tumbler is especially popular with Fiesta collectors, since the same gray is a standard Fiesta color from the '50s.

Plate 34

Juice Tumblers.

At first glance one might assume that these tumblers would be from the '50s, since rose and gray were standard '50s colors. But juice tumblers were discontinued well before then. Instead, the gray is actually Jubilee's Mist Gray and the rose a standard Harlequin color of the late '30s, "borrowed" to add a seventh color to the seven-piece juice set. The second pair of tumblers are glazed in Jubilee's Shell Pink and Cream Beige. You'll find variations in height as well as thickness, as you can see in comparing the pairs in the photo.

Plate 35

Juice pitchers in colors other than yellow and red are extremely rare. This one in turquoise, shown alongside its larger counterpart, is a one-of-a-kind example that recently sold for a staggering sum on a mail bid. One has been reported in light green and another in Jubilee Cream Beige. The juice pitcher measures 5¾" in height compared to the larger water pitcher that's 7¾" tall.

Plate 31

Plate 32

Plate 36

Disk Juice Pitcher, Juice Tumblers.

Of all the promotional items, the 30-oz. juice pitcher and 5-oz. tumblers are the only ones that are fairly easy to find. Nearly every pitcher you'll see will be yellow (collectors report a high incidence of the use of Harlequin yellow, a slightly brighter shade than Fiesta yellow), though on rare occasion you may find one in red. The red pitchers, according to a recent report by a couple who discovered some of the original coupons, were offered as a promotion by the Dayton Spice Mills, the Old Reliable Coffee Company. "Yours for only 3 coupons and $1.19," one says, "6 tumblers in lovely colors (it lists turquoise, green, yellow, blue, ivory, and red) "and a superbly shaped red Fiesta jug. High quality both in material and texture. . . designed and executed with artistic skill of the first order." And imagine finding a set with the original J.C. Penney price tag still attached — "98¢" for the "JCSET," "O.P.A." (Office of Price Administration, a price-control agency of the U.S. Government during WWII). Though juice tumblers were discontinued before the '50s, rose tumblers are not uncommon. Rose was a standard Harlequin color in the late '30s and was "borrowed" to add an extra touch of color to the set.

Plate 33

Plate 34

Plate 35

Plate 36

Plate 37

Disk Water Pitcher, Water Tumblers.

Not original but added to the line in 1939, the disk water pitcher continued to be made until the end of production. It's very scarce in medium green and chartreuse and rather hard to find in the '50s colors. The tumblers were discontinued between '44 and '46, having been made since the onset of production, so they're found in the original six colors only, with turquoise perhaps being a little scarce.

Plate 38

There are variations on the relish tray inserts, the most obvious is in the thickness of the walls. If you order one of these by mail, be sure to specify which you need, as they don't mix well and won't fit together properly. The thicker inserts are molded, so they usually carry the cast-indented mark — an integral part of the mold itself. The thinner ones were pressed by machine (a quicker and more economical method of production) and are usually not marked, though you will find some that are ink stamped. No doubt the thick ones are a little older, but this will have no bearing on value, at least to most collectors.

Plate 39

Relish Tray.

Five individual sections fit into the base of the relish tray. Its round center is often mistaken for a coaster, and though the company never produced them with that use in mind, it seems likely that at least some may have been bought for just that purpose, since we have had several reports from collectors who have found groups of them in old estates. Color make-up is important in determining the value of a relish tray. Red and cobalt are the most desirable base colors, and the more sections present in these colors, the higher the price.

2-Pint Jug.

The 2-pint jug (shown here in gray) was part of the original assortment. It was made until mid-'56, so it comes in all colors but medium green.

Ice Pitcher.

Made from 1936 until sometime between 1944 and '46 in the original colors only, the ice pitcher is a little hard to find in ivory, but it's red and turquoise that top the price scale. Though its looks seem to suggest otherwise, it does not take a lid.

Plate 37

Photo by Richard Wright

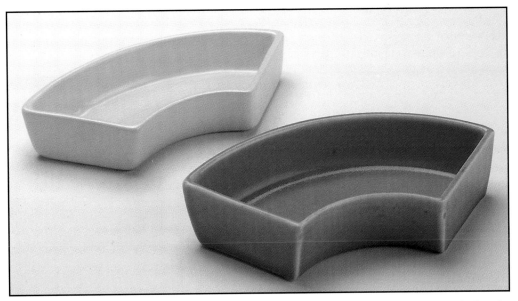

Photo by Richard Wright

Plate 38

Plate 39

Plate 40

Cake Plate.

The 10" cake plate is completely flat and very, very rare. We've never found it mentioned in any of the company's literature, but since it has been reported in all six original colors (one in ivory finally turned up), it has to be an early piece. One lucky collector's cake plate bears an original paper label that reads "Cake Kraft."

Plate 41

Deep Plate.

The deep plate was an August 1936 item that continued in production until the restyling — it's 8¾" diameter and found in all eleven colors. Most of us would call it a soup or salad bowl, though it is fairly shallow.

Plate 42

Though it's a little hard to believe considering the careful attention he paid to detail throughout the line, the syrup is the only piece of Fiesta that Rhead did not design. The mold was bought from the DripCut Company, who made the tops for HLC. (Other potteries, Vernon Kiln for one, also used this mold, and you'll find them in glass as well.) The blue one is molded of white ceramic and is marked "DripCut, Heatproof, L.A., Cal." The red one is genuine Fiesta. Decades ago a tea company filled syrup bases with tea leaves, added a cork stopper and their label, and unwittingly contributed to the frustration of today's collectors who have only a bottom. See the chapter entitled "Commercial Adaptations and Ephemera" for a photo.

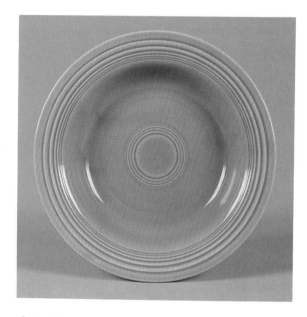

Plate 41

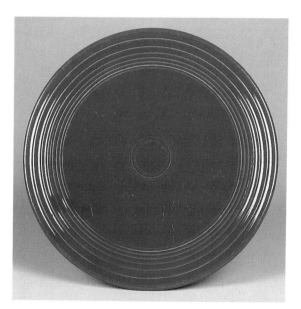

Plate 40

Plate 42

Plate 43
Sauce Boat.

 The sauce boat shown in this photo is from the original line, but the stand (underplate) didn't became available until the Ironstone line was introduced in 1969. Measuring 9" x 6½", the stand is relatively hard to find and makes a very desirable addition to any Fiesta collection.

Plate 44
Handled Chop Plate.

 This is how the chop plate was marketed in the '39-'43 selling campaign. It was offered along with seven other items at the very attractive price of $1.00 each. The rattan-wrapped handles were of course manufactured by another company and shipped to HLC where they were fitted to these plates. They have been found in sizes to fit the 7", 9", and 10" plates (this size also fits the relish tray) as well as the 13" and 15" chop plates.

Plate 43

Plate 44

Plate 45

Compartment Plate, 12".

These were made from 1936 until mid-'37. They're not mentioned on the May 1937 price list and have never been reported in turquoise. They measure 11½" (actual measurement for a 12" plate).

Compartment Plate, 10½".

Not quite as scarce, this size replaced the larger one in mid-'37. It was dropped in 1956, three years before the advent of medium green. These measure very close to the listed size.

Chop Plate, 15".

Both chop plates were in the original assortment. This one was discontinued early in 1956, so it is found in all colors except medium green. Actual measurement is 14¼".

Chop Plate, 13".

This size continued to be made until the restyling and can be found in all eleven colors, though it's rare in medium green. A black example was reported several years ago — well before the advent of the new black Fiesta. Both this size and the 15" chop plate will be found with a double foot ring. Though company officials today speculate that the second ring may have been added to act as a reinforcement, collectors have reported finding several of these double-ringed versions on metal Lazy-Susan bases in the original colors as well as in those of the '50s. We speculate that these were made on special order from a distributor who sold them as a unit with the metal base.

Plates, 10", 9", 7", 6".

Plates have always been in good supply, however the 10" size is becoming harder to find. The number of rings within the foot area on the back of any Fiesta plate will vary; these identified the particular jigging machine that made it and were used for quality control purposes. Occasionally you may notice when you stack your plates that not all are the same depth. If there was a purpose for this variation, we are not aware of it. From the 10" down to the 6" size, they're available in all eleven colors. (We recently had a report of a dinner plate in Harlequin spruce green.) They actually measure 10⅜", 9½", 7½", and 6½".

Plate 45

Plate 46

Sauce Boat.

The sauce boat (gravy boat) was produced from 1937 until 1973 in all of Fiesta's colors, with red and the colors of the '50s most difficult to find.

Platter.

The 12½" platter was first listed in July 1938 and continued in production until the restyling (Fiesta Ironstone) when it was enlarged to 13". It's easy to find in all eleven colors.

Utility Tray.

Added to the line in mid-'36, the utility tray (referred to as "celery tray" on Western price lists) continued in production until sometime between '44 and '46, so you'll find them in only the first six colors with red perhaps a bit hard to find.

Syrup.

Syrups rate very high with collectors. You'll find them in only the first six colors, and they're scarce in ivory.

Salt and Pepper Shakers.

These were made during the entire production period and can be found in all the Fiesta colors. Aside from the larger Kitchen Kraft shakers, this is the only style made in the Fiesta line. You may find a good imitation with holes on the side, but they are not genuine. Remember that Fiesta was widely copied, not only the bright glazes but often the band of rings as well. Though generally all shakers have the center hole, you'll find a few without. If this is an issue with you, yellow, medium green, and dark green "center holeless" shakers have been reported. Virtually all are unmarked; only a very few have been reported with the "HLCo USA" marking.

Plate 46

39

Plate 47

Teapot.

Notice that the medium green teapot has the vent hole in the lid, while the gray example does not. Vent holes required hand work, and occasionally you'll find a lid without a hole — whether by oversight or intention, we really don't know.

Plate 48

Teapot, Medium.

This size was added to the line in 1937 and was available throughout the entire production period. You'll find it in all eleven colors, though it's rare in medium green.

Teapot, Large.

This was in the original assortment. It was made only until sometime between '44 and '46, so it's found in just the first six colors.

Plate 49

Flower Vase, 8".

All three sizes of the flower vase were introduced in mid-'36 according to Rhead's magazine article we referenced back in the chapter entitled "The Story of Fiesta." They're all very scarce and highly valued by collectors. This size continued longest in production — it was dropped between '44 and '46.

Flower Vase, 10".

This size was made only from mid-'36 until Fall of 1942. One was recently found in ivory with red rings.

Vase, 12".

This size was discontinued along with the 10" vase by the Fall of 1942. All these vases are available in only the first six colors. One of our fondest memories is a visit to East Liverpool when we were just beginning to research the first Fiesta book, during the early 1970s. We found a little antique store well stocked with good Fiesta; among several other purchases we took home a pair of 12" vases in cobalt for $7.00 each.

Bud Vase.

Part of the original line, the bud vase was discontinued between '44 and '46. It's fairly easy to find and was made in the first six colors. An unusual example in black was reported several years ago (before '86 and not from the new line), another was found in the brown-mottled orange shown later in the "Experimentals and Employees' Inventions" chapter, and you may find a very similar design by Van Briggle. HLC's is 6¼" tall.

Plate 47

Plate 48

Plate 49

Plate 50
We thought you'd enjoy seeing this full-page shot of some nice medium green items. This color is scarce and is considered very desirable by collectors today. Prices continue to increase for even the smallest items. Some pieces of Fiesta are very rare in medium green, for instance: the cream soup (see Plate 51), 6" bowl, 4¾" fruit, disk pitcher, casserole, and medium teapot. And of course, since it was not introduced until '59 and many pieces had been discontinued by then, some items are simply not available in this color. Even to the most experienced eye, the difference between a heavy application of light green and average coverage in medium green is sometimes a bit tricky to discern.

Plate 50

Plate 51
Cream Soup.

Most collectors, if they could choose any piece of Fiesta, would want one of these — a medium green cream soup!

Plate 52
Fruit Bowls.

Over the past few years, we've had many newcomers who have asked for some help in sorting out all those greens. We hope these fruit bowls will visually "fill the bill." Left to right the colors are: chartreuse, medium green, light green, and dark green.

Plate 51

Plate 52

Fiesta Ironstone

In 1969 Fiesta was restyled, and the line that was offered in February of the following year was called Fiesta Ironstone. There were many factors that of necessity brought about this change. Labor and production costs had risen sharply. Efforts to hold these costs down resulted in the use of two new colors which were standard for several other lines of dinnerware produced at HLC: Antique Gold and Turf Green. This eliminated the need of the separate firing that had been necessary for the older Fiesta colors. It was pointed out to us as we toured the factory that since each color required different temperatures in the kiln, orders were running ahead of production for Fiesta as well as their other lines. In order to cut labor cost, all markings were eliminated. (You will very seldom find an item with the Fiesta stamp; this was never the practice, and such pieces must be from early in the transition.)

The restyled pieces had a more contemporary feeling — bowls were flared, and the applied handles were only partial rings. The covered casserole had molded, closed handles, and the handles had been eliminated entirely from the sugar bowl. The covered coffee server made a return appearance after an absence of several years. Twenty-two items were offered in three colors: Antique Gold, Turf Green, and the original red, now called Mango Red. The oval platter was enlarged from 12" to 13"; three new items were offered, the soup/cereal, the sauce boat stand, and the 10" salad bowl.

Finally in November 1972, all production of Fiesta red was discontinued because many of the original technicians who developed this color and maintained control over the complicated manufacturing and firing had retired, and modern mass-production methods were unsuited to the process. On January 1, 1973, the famous line of Fiesta dinnerware was discontinued altogether.

Because Ironstone was made for a relatively short time, it is not easy to find. But since the old Fiesta line has become so costly to collect, enthusiasm for the Ironstone has recently begun to generate. Red mugs and the sauce boat stand in any color are regarded as "good pieces." Red is the most difficult color to find; green is scarce in some pieces, and gold is the most available. You may find cups with the Ironstone handle in Fiesta yellow, medium green, and turquoise. (For a complete listing of available items, see "Suggested Values" in the back of the book.)

Plate 53

44

Fiesta Kitchen Kraft

Since the early 1930s, the Homer Laughlin China Company had been well known as manufacturers of a wide variety of ceramic kitchenwares. In 1939 they introduced a bake-and-serve line called Fiesta Kitchen Kraft as an extension of their already popular genuine Fiesta ware. This they offered in four original Fiesta colors — red, yellow, green, and blue. The following pieces (compiled from the April 1941 price list) were available:

Covered jars: small, medium, and large
Mixing bowls: 10", 8", and 6"
Covered casseroles: 8½", 7½", and individual
Pie plate, 10"
Salt and pepper shakers, large

Covered jug, large
Spoon, fork, and cake server
Refrigerator set, 4-pc.
Cake plate, 11"
Plates: 6" and 9"

These were chosen from the standard assortment of kitchenware items which had been the basis of the many Kitchen Kraft and OvenServe decaled lines of years previous; none were created especially for Fiesta Kitchen Kraft. This line was in production for a relatively short period — perhaps being discontinued sometime during WWII prior to 1945.

In addition to the items listed previously, there are at least three more to add. These may have been offered in the original assortment and discontinued by the 1941 listing. They are the oval platter in a chrome holder (which was shipped as a unit from HLC); a 9" pie plate; and a variation in size of the covered jug. The difference is so slight, even side by side it could go unnoticed. Collectors report as many of one size as the other. If you really want to label yours large or small, check the circumference. The larger one measures 21½" while the smaller one is 20".

The 6" and 9" plates listed on the 1941 illustrated brochure were used as underplates for the casseroles. When we visited the morgue at HLC); we saw an example of these. They were of a thinner gauge and seemed to have been taken from one of their other lines, since the style was not typical. They were round and had a moderately wide, slightly flared rim. They're very, very rare in Fiesta KK colors; only recently have we heard from a collector who sent us a photograph of a light green example. (See the color plate on page 47.)

If you have been interested at all in the decaled lines, you are probably familiar enough with the Kitchen Kraft molds that you recognize them easily. Several collectors have mentioned finding their stack set, salt and peppers, mixing bowls, and other items in an ivory glaze; but as far as we can determine from any information available, ivory was never listed as a Fiesta Kitchen Kraft color, so these are rare. Of the four standard colors, dark blue is most in demand and, along with red, represents the high side of the price range.

Plates 54

Casserole Variations.

  This casserole has a base with variations from the standard mold in that the lip is recessed, and this one has no mark. The lid is shown here in detail.

Plates 55

Individual Casserole and Underplate.

  The underplate beneath the individual casserole measures 6½" in diameter. This was the first one we'd ever heard of, but since we received this photo, a second underplate has been reported as well.

Plates 56

Covered Jar.

  Photo shows detail of lid. See graduated sizes in Plate 59.

Plate 57

Casseroles.

  These come in three sizes: 8½", 7½", and individual. All are scarce. In Plate 54 you'll see the lid in greater detail.

Plate 58

Mixing Bowls.

  The mixing bowls measure 10", 8", and 6" and have proven rather difficult to find. Note the original sticker on the large one. They have been found in white as well as Harlequin, Jubilee, and Rhythm colors. Such bowls may or may not be marked. Although a kitchenware bowl seems an unlikely liquor decanter, the 6" size has been reported with this message in gold lettering: "This whiskey is 4 years old, 90 proof Maryland straight rye whiskey, Wm. Jameson, Inc., N.Y., Shorewood, the finest name in rye."

Plate 54

Plate 55

Plate 56

Plate 57

Plate 58

Plate 59

Covered Jars.

To determine the size of your covered jar, measure the circumference. The large jar is 27½" around, the medium 22", and the small one is 14½". These make lovely (though unhandy) canisters in a vintage kitchen. Lid detail is evident in Plate 56.

Plate 60

Servers: Spoon, Cake Lifter, Fork.

These are hard to find, especially in mint condition. Their handles are decorated with the same embossed flowers as one of the OvenServe lines. Plate 65 shows the completed collection displayed to full advantage. In Plate 61, alongside a green fork, is another version of the spoon; this one is very rare indeed. It's slightly more narrow and 11½" long.

Salt and Pepper Shakers.

These are larger replicas of their Fiesta dinnerware counterparts, although by no means as plentiful. You may on rare occasions find them glazed in Harlequin yellow.

Plate 59

Plate 60

Plate 61

Spoon Variation and Fork.

This is another version of the serving spoon, very rare indeed. It's slightly more narrow and 11½" long. As far as we know, there are two of these in ivory, one in white, one with decals, and another in turquoise, which the owner says came from the Wells' estate. He also tells us that he has seen a brochure from Homer Laughlin that shows a light green one. We've heard only rumors of a fork and pie server in a size that corresponds. We would enjoy hearing from anyone who has information on these items.

Plate 62

Covered Jug.

There are two sizes in these jugs, but the differences are subtle. The circumference of the larger is 21½"; the smaller measures 20" around.

Plate 63

Stack Set (Refrigerator Jars).

The covered refrigerator stack set consists of three units and a flat lid and are usually made up of all four Kitchen Kraft colors. A rare few components and one whole unit have been found in the ivory line. An ivory lid exists with the original Kitchen Kraft label. No, trust me — these are not dog dishes.

Plate 61

Plate 63

Plate 62

Plate 64

Cake Plate.

These may or may not be marked — one example has been reported with a gold ink stamped "Fiesta HLC." The only decoration is the narrow band around the edge formed by one indented ring. They are much easier to find than the regular Fiesta cake plate.

Pie Plates.

These come in two sizes: 10" and 9". Actually they measure 10¼" and 9¾". (Read the chapter "Dating Codes and English Measurements" if you're as confused as we once were.) They were produced without rings either inside or outside and are usually not marked, though we have one with a gold Fiesta stamp. The 10" size has been reported in the maroon and spruce green of the Harlequin line. In the chapter called "Go-Alongs," you'll see the metal frame (similar to the one in Plate 66) that was sometimes shipped along with the pie plates directly from the factory. It is very unusual to find the small size in the Fiesta KK colors; it is more often found in ivory decorated with decals.

Plate 65

Servers: Spoon, Cake Lifter, Fork.

This is a completed collection displayed to full advantage. Since the last edition of our book, a spoon has been reported in dark green and a cake lifter in turquoise.

Plate 66

Platter.

This is the 13" oval platter, shown in Harlequin spruce green, not a Fiesta Kitchen Kraft color. These are very, very rare in this color. A few have been found in Harlequin yellow, and one has been reported in mauve blue. Even in the regular four colors, these are scarce. They're not usually marked. The metal holder is an HLC issue, though of course not all of these platters were sold in a frame.

Plate 64

Plate 65

Plate 66

GENUINE

Fiesta

H. L. Co. USA
CASUAL

There were two designs produced in the beautiful Fiesta Casuals; and although they are both relatively difficult to find, often when they are found the set may be complete, or nearly so. They were introduced in June 1962; and as sales were only moderately active, they were discontinued around 1968. The Plaid Stamp Company featured both lines in their illustrated catalogs during these years.

The Hawaiian 12-Point Daisy design featured a ½" turquoise band at the rim and turquoise daisies with brown centers on a white background. The other pattern was Yellow Carnation which featured the yellow flowers with a touch of brown on white background. A yellow rim band completed the design. In each line, only the dinner plates, salad plates, saucers, and oval platters were decorated; the cups, fruit dishes, nappies, sugar bowls, and creamers were simply glazed in the matching Fiesta color. The designs were hand sprayed and overglazed using a lead mask with the cut-out motif. A complete service consisted of six place settings: dinner plate, salad plate, cup and saucer, and 5½" fruit. A platter, 8½" nappy, and the sugar and creamer were also included. (For a listing of available items, see "Suggested Values" in back of book.)

Plate 67

Plate 67
Hawaiian 12-Point Daisy Design.

Plate 68
Yellow Carnation Design.

Plate 68

Fiesta with Stripes

We have no information concerning the decorator of this line of striped Fiesta, but newly discovered covered onion soup bowls (one from a spectacular set of eight is shown in Plate 70) indicate it must have been done sometime before the Fall of 1937 (much earlier than we could first pinpoint it), since that's when the onion soups were discontinued. You'll see a coffeepot with blue stripes in Plate 69, and in addition to the items shown, a large comport, 10" vase, footed salad bowl, and bulb and tripod candle holders have also been reported. So far, red and blue stripes are all that have surfaced, and by far the majority is in red. This dinnerware is very rare. The stripes are well done and generally show no wear, but are not underglaze as we originally assumed. You may find some plates with stripes that are over the glaze and poorly applied (one at the rim and another inside the band of rings); these are usually very worn and have little value.

Plate 69
Coffeepot.

Plate 70
Onion Soup Bowl.

Plate 71
Set of Eight.

Plate 69

Plate 70

Plate 71

Photo © Adam Anik

Fiesta with Decals

Here and on the following pages are examples of Fiesta with decals. You'll find other examples not shown. They may have been decorated by HLC, but more than likely the work was done by smaller decorating companies — there were several in the immediate vicinity. We are sure that the turkey plates shown in Plate 72 were done by Homer Laughlin. According to the company, commercial grade ware was used for this line. These are rare.

The floral dinnerware in Plate 73 is only one example of many — you'll find various decals, and some may be trimmed with bands or stripes around the rims. This type of dinnerware is very rare, and to rebuild a matching set would be next to impossible.

Becoming an area of collecting interest all its own, the decal of the 18th-century couple in a garden setting was used not only to decorate some of HLC's lines but other pottery companies' as well. The decorating on many of these items was done by Royal China, who often added their mark to that of the pottery company. HLC's Georgian line has been found with this decal, so have items marked W.S. George, and there are many others. In past editions we have featured cake sets made up of the 15" Fiesta chop plate and six matching dessert plates — one set in ivory, a second in yellow. This decal has not been limited to dinnerware; you'll often see lamps, vases, and other assorted pieces with variations of this theme. More often than not, decals were applied on the ivory glaze.

Relish trays seem to have been a favorite item with decorating firms, as we have seen several; the one in Plate 77 is especially attractive. HLC issued calendar plates for a number of years, using whatever blanks were available. In 1954 and 1955, they just happened to use Fiesta, as shown in Plate 81.

Plate 72

Very Rare Turkey Plates.
    Shown are the 9" plate with a maroon band, a 13" chop plate with a yellow band, and the Kitchen Kraft cake plate trimmed in gold. The 15" chop plate has also been reported with the turkey decal, as has a Rhythm platter.

Plate 72

Plate 73

Example of Floral Dinnerware.

This type of dinnerware is very rare. It can be found with various decals; some may be trimmed with bands or stripes around the rims.

Plate 74

Demitasse Cup and Saucer Set.

Notice the elaborate gold tracing in this example with an 18th-century couple in a garden setting.

Plate 75

8½" Nappy.

This is from another line—the decal is the same, but this one has maroon stripes on the rim.

Plate 73

Plate 74

Plate 75

Plate 76
Chop Plate.
   Shown here decorated with eight gold butterflies and gold rim stripes, this chop plate makes an unusual tidbit tray with the addition of the handle.

Plate 77
Relish Tray.
   An especially attractive example.

Plate 78
Sweets Comport.
   Another example of floral-decorated Fiesta, this one well trimmed in gold.

Plate 79
Ashtray.
   Shown in the blue of Skytone. The decal is called Stardust. These blue lines were popular sellers during the '40s and '50s.

Plate 76

Plate 77

Plate 78

Plate 79

Plate 80

Tom and Jerry Mugs and Footed Salad Bowl.
   Shown in ivory trimmed with gold bands and lettering to make a T&J set that is very hard to find complete; bowls are more difficult to locate than mugs. You'll more often find another set; it's by HLC as well, but it's not on the Fiesta mold. These are listed in the Fiesta price guide, along with the set shown here, and shown in the "Miscellaneous" chapter.

Plate 81

Calendar Plates.
   The 9" plate in the center is the rare size; it may be found for either 1954 or 1955. The 1954 plate has been found in ivory only; the '55 may be green, yellow, or ivory.

Plate 80

Plate 81

New Fiesta

After a 13-year absence, Fiesta was reintroduced to the market on February 28, 1986. Its Art Deco style, which had looked somewhat dated in 1973 when the Fiesta Ironstone line was discontinued, had again become the rage in home decoration. Only a short time before this, several lines of solid color dinnerware had been introduced by competitors (including Moderna by Mikasa and line-for-line interpretation of Fiesta by Rego China made for the restaurant trade), and these were enjoying enough success to convince Homer Laughlin to test the waters. Sample items were produced and dipped in a number of colors to gauge consumer preferences at a Chicago trade show in December 1985. A gray and yellow was also tested in addition to the five winning colors of Cobalt Blue (darker and denser than the original), Rose (a true pink), White, Apricot (a pale peach), and Black. Interest was deemed great enough to begin production. A last-minute decision to go with a vitrified body (as opposed to the semivitrified clay used for the original Fiesta) was made in order to appeal to the restaurant trade. While vitrified china is denser and will not absorb moisture, it has to be fired at a higher temperature and shrinks more during firing. Because of this, new molds had to be designed for the dinner plates to keep them at 10½". The higher firing also caused some shapes to have a tendency to deform. Thus the Ironstone-style casserole, sugar bowl, coffee server, and flat teapot lid had to be redesigned. The original brochures used photographs of the semivitrified samples and showed the Ironstone-style handled casserole. But this particular item was never produced in the new line; instead it was restyled into the covered casserole shown in Plate 82. The coffee server was replaced by the restyled version (see Plate 84 for both styles — the restyle is in the foreground). Today the original style has a market value of approximately $125.00. Note the differences in the finials. The original had the Ironstone-type knob, while the restyle has the more familiar flared knob from the old Fiesta line. This detail was eventually changed on virtually every item in the line that took a lid. The sugar bowl was replaced with one made from the old marmalade mold (without the notch for the spoon) in the first few months of production.

Plate 82

A warm, sunny Southwestern atmosphere is created here by Apricot (casserole, chop plate, disk pitcher, etc.); new Turquoise (medium flower vase, butter dish, platter); new Yellow (tripod candle holders, cup and saucer); and Sea Mist Green (coffee mug). If you have trouble deciding whether your cobalt and turquoise tripods are old or new, take a look at their bases. If they are fully glazed, they're old. Turquoise, Cobalt, and Sapphire are generally the new colors most difficult to distinguish from the old. If you can't compare colors, remember that sagger pin marks indicate old Fiesta (Homer Laughlin just doesn't use them anymore), new foot rings are shiny, and the ink stamp has been altered (see the line drawing on page 60). Only those pieces that were made from the old, original molds carry the old in-mold mark. (The company is planning to change this, however; see information top of page 61. They've also announced plans to eventually convert all marks to the ink-stamped "lead free" insignia.)

Plate 82

GENUINE

H•L•Co

U.S.A.

Seven new colors have been added to the original lineup — Turquoise (darker, with more of a green cast than the old color); Yellow (very pale); Periwinkle Blue (pastel gray-blue); Sea Mist Green (pale mint green, 1991); a limited line in Lilac (a rich, deep tone produced for only two years, 1994 and 1995); and a regular-line color called Persimmon (a reddish coral shade, early 1996). An additional limited edition color called Sapphire (a bright electric blue — slightly lighter and more brilliant than the 1930s cobalt) was produced exclusively for Bloomingdale's during the Winter of 1996. Unlike the Lilac which was produced for a full two years, Sapphire (according to Bloomingdale's, anyway) was limited to 180 firing days.

Homer Laughlin has announced that Apricot will be discontinued after December 1997. They tell us that Black will be placed on "non-stock status," meaning it will only be produced to order several times a year and will require a longer lead time for orders, rather than being produced and carried in stock. This will allow them to add additional colors to the line without having to further discontinue slower selling colors or add more glaze mills and spray line equipment. These ten items will no longer be available in Black: napkin rings, clock, medium vase, coffee server, handled carafe, bud vase, round (bulb) candle holders, after dinner cup and saucer, pyramid (tripod) candle holders, and the small disk pitcher.

Many items have been added to the line since 1986, some of them designed for the restaurant trade. The original 1986 assortment of pieces as well as some (not all) subsequent additions are shown on the company flyer on pages 62 and 63. To help identify the new colors, we've also shown the flyer front.

The items marked with an asterisk (*) in the following list have been added since the 1986 reintroduction.

After Dinner Cup and Saucer*
Bouillon Cup, 4" *
Bread and Butter Plate, 6½" *
Bud Vase
Bulb Candle Holders
Cake Plate/Serving Tray, 11"*
Cereal Bowl, 5½" *
Chop Plate, 12"
Coffee Mug, 10-oz. *
Coffee Server
Covered Butter Dish*
Covered Casserole
Covered Teapot
Cup
Dinner Plate, 10½"
Fruit Bowl, 5¼" *
Large Disk Pitcher
Luncheon Plate, 9" *
Medium Flower Vase, 9½"
Miniature Disk Pitcher, 5-oz. *
Napkin Ring*
Oval Platter, 9½"*
Oval Platter, 11½"*

Oval Platter, 13½"*
Pie Baker, 10"*
Pyramid (tripod) Candle Holders
Redesigned Carafe (no stopper)*
Regular Covered Sugar
Regular Creamer
Relish Dish (corn-on-the-cob server)*
Rimmed Soup (centerpiece bowl), 12"*
Rimmed Soup (deep plate)*
Salad Plate, 7⅛"
Salt and Pepper
Sauce Boat
Saucer
Serving Bowl, 32-oz.
Small Disk Pitcher
Soup/Cereal Bowl, 6⅞"
Stacking Cereal Bowl, 6½"*
Sugar and Creamer on Figure-Eight Tray
Table Lamp (J.C. Penney Exclusive), 1993*
Tumbler, 6½-oz.*
Wall Clock (produced in 1993, discontinued, then reintroduced in 1966)*

Other items are being introduced as retailers request them. All of the pieces in the previous listing are marked Fiesta (including cups) with the exception of the butter dish. The cast-indented mark is very similar to the old; the ink-stamped items are marked with a new version (see line drawing). Eventually the company's intentions are to replace all cast-indented marks with an ink stamp, similar to the line drawing shown on page 60 but including the words "lead free" and a dating code, all within a circular reserve.

Because there was so much variation in the old turquoise shades, the new turquoise is the only color likely to cause any confusion to collectors of the old, and only then when it is not compared to an old, original piece. Almost all the new items will be slightly smaller and feel heavier than the old, due to the vitrified clay. In addition, all new items will have a wiped (or dry, unglazed) foot versus a glazed foot, and you will notice a shine to the wiped area. (The new items sit directly on the kiln shelf and so cannot be glazed on the contact points.) If an item has three sagger pin marks, it is almost certainly old, since the company no longer uses them. In addition to the above items, Homer Laughlin has added several items to the line which are standard HLC restaurant shapes dipped in Fiesta glazes and sold under the name "Fiesta Mates." These items will generally not have the concentric rings or other elements typical of Fiesta styling and will be marked with the Homer Laughlin backstamp rather than the Fiesta backstamp shown previously. They include:

Jumbo 18-oz. Bowl
  (often called a "Chili Bowl")
Jumbo 18-oz. Cup and Saucer
Skillet Server
Irish Coffee Mug

Tower Mug
Denver Mug
Colonial Teapot, 18½-oz.
Oval Baker, 10"

Sugar Caddy
  (sweetener packet holder)
Seville Ramekin, 3½-oz.
Creamer Jug, 15¼-oz.

Plate 83

The new Cobalt is much darker than either the original 1936 cobalt or the new limited edition Sapphire. Just how dark is evident in the juice pitcher at the left of the picture. The oval platter is Black and the bulb candlesticks White. Both old and new bulb candlesticks have a dry foot. Remember to look for the shine, the mark, and try to learn to recognize the new colors. The large pasta bowl (center back) is in Periwinkle; the gravy boat is Rose. In 1986 when it was introduced, Rose was the lighter, baby pink shown here. In the past several years, HLC has been slowly making it a deeper and richer tone; it's now almost a hot pink, which becomes especially obvious if you try to add to a set purchased ten years ago.

Plate 83

FIESTA COLORS

| F-100 WHITE | F-101 BLACK | F-103 ROSE | F-104 APRICOT | F-105 COBALT BLUE | F-106 YELLOW | F-107 TURQUOISE | F-108 PERIWINKLE BLUE | F-109 SEA MIST GREEN | F-114 PERSIMMON |

The Homer Laughlin China Co.
Newell, W. Va. 26050
Made in USA

1-800-452-4462   FAX 304-387-0593

Front of Company Flyer.

Courtesy Homer Laughlin China Co.

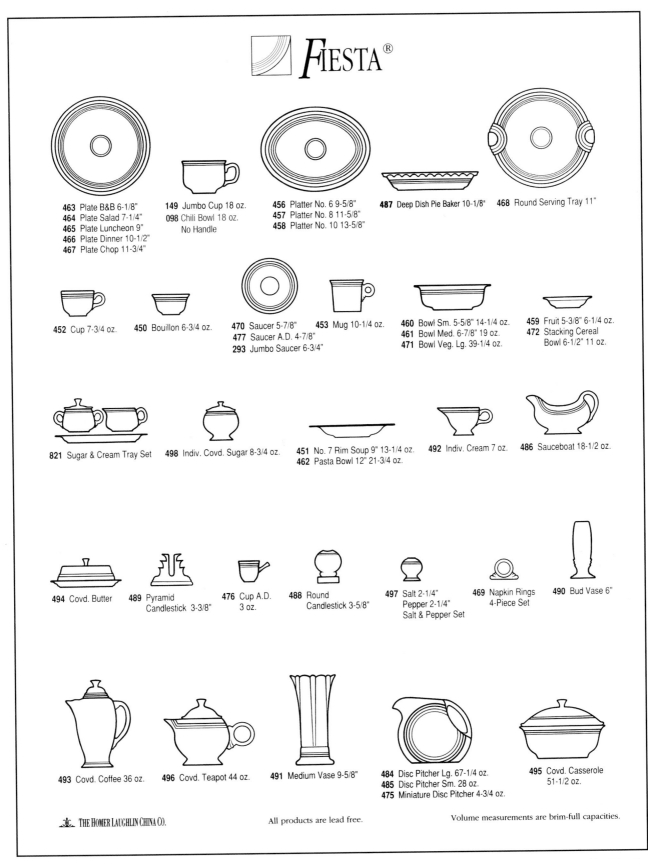

FIESTA ®

463 Plate B&B 6-1/8"
464 Plate Salad 7-1/4"
465 Plate Luncheon 9"
466 Plate Dinner 10-1/2"
467 Plate Chop 11-3/4"

149 Jumbo Cup 18 oz.
098 Chili Bowl 18 oz.
No Handle

456 Platter No. 6 9-5/8"
457 Platter No. 8 11-5/8"
458 Platter No. 10 13-5/8"

487 Deep Dish Pie Baker 10-1/8"

468 Round Serving Tray 11"

452 Cup 7-3/4 oz.

450 Bouillon 6-3/4 oz.

470 Saucer 5-7/8"
477 Saucer A.D. 4-7/8"
293 Jumbo Saucer 6-3/4"

453 Mug 10-1/4 oz.

460 Bowl Sm. 5-5/8" 14-1/4 oz.
461 Bowl Med. 6-7/8" 19 oz.
471 Bowl Veg. Lg. 39-1/4 oz.

459 Fruit 5-3/8" 6-1/4 oz.
472 Stacking Cereal
Bowl 6-1/2" 11 oz.

821 Sugar & Cream Tray Set

498 Indiv. Covd. Sugar 8-3/4 oz.

451 No. 7 Rim Soup 9" 13-1/4 oz.
462 Pasta Bowl 12" 21-3/4 oz.

492 Indiv. Cream 7 oz.

486 Sauceboat 18-1/2 oz.

494 Covd. Butter

489 Pyramid
Candlestick 3-3/8"

476 Cup A.D.
3 oz.

488 Round
Candlestick 3-5/8"

497 Salt 2-1/4"
Pepper 2-1/4"
Salt & Pepper Set

469 Napkin Rings
4-Piece Set

490 Bud Vase 6"

493 Covd. Coffee 36 oz.

496 Covd. Teapot 44 oz.

491 Medium Vase 9-5/8"

484 Disc Pitcher Lg. 67-1/4 oz.
485 Disc Pitcher Sm. 28 oz.
475 Miniature Disc Pitcher 4-3/4 oz.

495 Covd. Casserole
51-1/2 oz.

THE HOMER LAUGHLIN CHINA CO.

All products are lead free.

Volume measurements are brim-full capacities.

Courtesy Homer Laughlin China Co.

Back of Company Flyer.

Plate 84

The coffeepot in the background was the original design, but due to warping problems resulting from the new clay, it was only produced for a short time. Collectors value this piece at $125.00 and up. The restyled version is in the foreground.

Plate 85

Note the difference in the lids. The teapot at the top of the photo has the Ironstone-like knob, while the bottom example has the flared finial from the original Fiesta line. Though the intention was to use the knob, it was eventually replaced by the flared finial on virtually every item in the new line that required a lid.

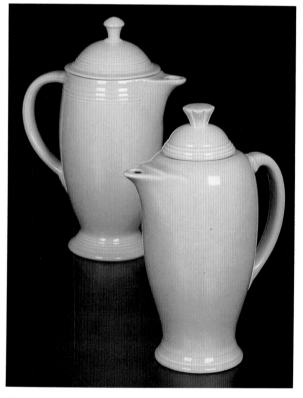

Plate 84

Plate 85

Lilac Fiesta has the distinction of being the first new Fiesta color to be discontinued. It was made for two years only (1994 and 1995), in virtually every item except the lamp, clock, and restyled carafe. Collectors pursue it with fervor. The camp is divided, however, between those who have complete confidence that it will never be reinstated and those who are unconvinced. The former collectors are willing to pay very substantial prices for the better items, while the latter believe it may be too soon to speculate where this market is going. To further make it unstable, some dealers who have been able to stockpile Lilac (often by buying warehouse overstock) are holding on to their merchandise, waiting to see what will happen. Generally, to give you an idea of the market during the fall of 1997, a five-piece plate setting sold for about $35.00, the small disk pitcher for $30.00, the flower vase around $200.00, the bud vase about $60.00, and the coffeepot and teapot at about $80.00 each. Tripod candle holders (a Bloomingdale's exclusive) were made in very limited numbers and at one point asking prices became astronomical. At a show and sale in 1997, a pair was offered for $400.00, though they didn't sell. Please don't feel that we endorse these values. For the most part, at least for now, we'll leave it up to each collector to decide what percentage or multiple of the suggested retail price they are willing to pay for Lilac.

Here is a sampling of the company's suggested net retail for Lilac: (Virtually all retailers discounted these prices.) Rim Soup, $10.40; Mug, 10", $10.50; 5-pc. Place Setting, $33.00; 20-pc. Set, $119.95; Chop Plate, 11½", $16.40; Large Vegetable Bowl, $11.40; Mini Disk Pitcher, $13.28; Large Disk Pitcher, $24.60; Sauce Boat, $21.90; Butter Dish, $20.00; Teapot, $29.00; Salt and Pepper Set, $13.75; Sugar, Creamer, and Tray Set, $31.95.

Plate 86

Relish Tray.

The relish tray (corn-on-the-cob server) is an innovative design; they retailed at about $20.00 at the outlet.

Plate 87

Disk Pitcher.

Homer Laughlin produced 60th anniversary commemorative items for 1996; this disk pitcher was part of a five-piece beverage set. They were produced in Lilac as well as six other colors: Turquoise, Cobalt, Periwinkle, Rose, Persimmon, and Sapphire.

Rose sets were made in very limited number (possibly less than three hundred, though there's no way to be exact), and at the time of this writing, Bloomingdale's claimed Sapphire would be limited to only 180 firing days. Sets normally retailed at about $50.00, though closeout/overstock prices were nearer $30.00.

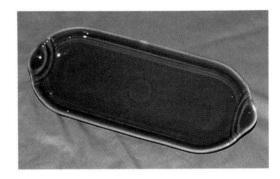

Plate 88

Tripod Candle Holders.

Here are the "infamous" Lilac tripod candle holders. These have attracted more interest than any other Lilac item since they were made in limited quantity. Collectors have paid dearly for a pair to call their own! These were a Bloomingdale's exclusive.

Plate 86

Plate 87

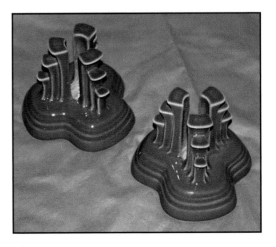

Plate 88

Plates 89 and 90

The bulb candle holders and bud vase were made especially for China Specialties, the after-dinner cup and saucer for both Bloomingdale's and China Specialties. As Homer Laughlin traditionally gives only a six-month exclusive on such items, some of these pieces may have been made for other retailers as well during the two-year production period.

Plate 91

Here are the two newest colors in the Fiesta line, Persimmon and the special limited edition Sapphire Blue made exclusively for Bloomingdale's. Note the medium flower vase and the newly restyled carafe in Sapphire Blue. (You may hear an exact number relative to how many vases were made, but according to contacts there, it's really impossible to say with certainty. It is safe to say that they will be hard to find in time to come.) Sapphire is slightly lighter and more brilliant than the old 1936 cobalt, and much lighter than the regular 1986 cobalt, which is an inky, almost black, cobalt blue. These are the items that are to be made in Sapphire: 5-pc. place settings, 13½" oval platter, 32-oz. serving bowl, large disk pitcher, 6½-oz. tumbler, clock, medium flower vase, serving tray, the newly restyled carafe, and from the Fiesta Mates line, you'll find the jumbo 18-oz. cup and saucer.

Plate 89

Plate 90

Plate 91

Plate 92

Assortment of items from the Fiesta Mates line.

    This line lacks the typical Fiesta styling; these pieces were taken from the regular restaurant line and dipped in Fiesta glazes. From left: sugar packet holder, fry pan server, 18-oz. jumbo cup and saucer, 4-oz. ramekin, 18-oz. jumbo bowl, 5-oz. creamer, Tower and Denver mugs, and the 10" oval baker.

Plate 93

Fiesta Flatware.

    The Fiesta flatware set consists of a dinner and salad fork, a tea and soup spoon, and a dinner knife, shown here in Lilac. The Hostess set (on the left) consists of a pie lifter, slotted and regular serving spoons, and a cold meat fork. An example of the steak knife is shown in Periwinkle (in the center). The flatware was made in all the colors listed for the dinnerware except Sapphire. Lilac was made in place setting items only — no serving pieces. In addition, a true red as well as emerald green were made to coordinate with the Holiday Fiesta shown in Plate 96. The flatware is marked Fiesta on the stainless steel tang.

Plate 92

Plate 93

Plate 94

Napkin Dispenser, Napkins, and Tablecloth.

Homer Laughlin has licensed several companies to make various accessory items. Here you see a metal diner-type napkin dispenser and paper napkins printed with a Fiesta plate design. Also shown is a fabric tablecloth produced by Dakotah for a limited time, 1994 to 1995. The fabric accessories were available in a scatter print as well as an allover plate design. In addition to tablecloths, Dakotah also made chair pads, curtains, decorator pillows, placemats, and napkins. All items were available in the "Original Color" version as well as a pastel-colored print to coordinate with the new Fiesta color assortment.

Plate 95

Fiesta Easel Sign.

A special item made for collectors, this Fiesta easel sign is to be made in a different color each year, exclusively for members of the Fiesta Collector's Quarterly. The 1995 color was Persimmon; the 1996 color was Turquoise. This is an example of the 60th anniversary commemoratives (all limited to six hundred pieces) that were made for subscribers in 1996. The decal was recreated for them from original advertising brochure artwork and is permanently fired on. These may be found with a subscriber's name inscribed in gold under the base along with a serial number. This type of sign is typical of advertising signs glass and china companies made for use in department store shelf and window displays during the 1950s.

Plate 94

Plate 95

Plates 96 and 97
First and second generations of Holiday Fiesta.
   The original line (sans the ribbon, Plate 97) was produced for the 1987 Christmas season only and was not a huge success; the revised line, currently offered by Homer Laughlin, has a larger decal and features a red ribbon in addition to the holly and berry motif. (Much better!) Homer Laughlin also plans to introduce a yearly Fiesta Christmas ornament, shaped like a miniature Fiesta plate. The 1997 ornament will feature the same holly decoration used on the Holiday Fiesta in Plate 96.

Plate 96

Plate 97

Plate 98

Fiesta for Warner Brothers and Macy's Department Store.

HLC has produced Fiesta place settings and serving pieces for Warner Brothers stores which feature a different Looney Tunes character for each color. There is Daffy Duck on Turquoise, Bugs Bunny on Periwinkle, Porky Pig on Rose, Sylvester on Yellow, and Tweety Bird on White. Others may follow. These items have become very popular with collectors, but we've recently learned that only one store will continue to carry Looney Tunes made from the Fiesta molds. The line that will appear in the Warner catalog will be on another shape. On the right is a decoration produced exclusively for Macy's Department Stores. It features White Fiesta with Persimmon, Periwinkle, Yellow and Sea Mist Green banding at the rim.

Plate 99

Lamp and Clock.

The Fiesta lamp (shown with its original shade). Produced in 1993 as a J.C. Penney exclusive, it met with little success and was offered for one season only. To the right is the clock. It too was a Penney's exclusive in 1993. It was discontinued but has recently been reintroduced as a regular line item available from all retailers.

Plate 98

Plate 99

Plate 100

Custom Designed Fiesta.

You will be seeing Fiesta items that have been custom decorated by Homer Laughlin and other firms that specialize in custom work. Many examples of Fiesta are custom crested with a restaurant name or special motifs for restaurants and hotels. In addition to wares such as these, HLC has designed exclusive decorations specifically with the collector in mind. Prior to the 1986 reintroduction of Fiesta, Homer Laughlin produced a limited edition Commemorative Fiesta 50th Anniversary Collector's Mug set for a private company, China Specialties, Inc. Fewer than six hundred sets were produced, each consisting of ten white mugs decorated with the Fiesta dancing senorita trademark, one in each of these Fiesta colors: red, yellow, cobalt, turquoise, light green, forest green, rose, chartreuse, gray, and medium green. Later, Homer Laughlin also brought out a collector/dealer sign, a white 12" chop plate with the Fiesta logo in Mango Red. A relative few were produced in yellow and apricot with Mango Red decoration. Shown here, the large pitcher is a limited edition of six hundred decorated with a fired-on decal modeled after an original advertisement for Fiesta. It was made for members of the Fiesta Collector's Quarterly. The mug is crested with a logo for the Tamarack resort, and you will find mugs carrying logos of the International House of Pancakes and other restaurant chains. The calendar plate was produced for a private company in 1993, and the pink flamingo pattern fired onto black Fiesta is called "Moon Over Miami." It is available only from an antique mall near the HLC plant.

Plate 101

60th Anniversary Commemorative Items.

Homer Laughlin produced a number of these special items to celebrate Fiesta's anniversary in 1996. The logo emblazoned on these items reads "Genuine Fiesta, 60th Anniversary, 1936–1996, still proudly made in the U.S.A. by the Homer Laughlin China Company." The five-piece beverage set was made in a number of colors: Persimmon, Lilac, Periwinkle, Turquoise, Cobalt, Rose, and Sapphire (see Plate 87 for more information). The mugs were available in Persimmon and White in addition to the Yellow and Turquoise shown. The round serving tray in the background is a new item, but one we feel Rhead would approve. The anniversary clock on the right features the special logo instead of the dancing senorita.

Plate 100

Plate 101

Editor's note: We're very grateful to Joel Wilson (China Specialties, Inc.; Fiesta Collector's Quarterly; Hall China Collector Club Newsletter) for supplying us with this up-to-date information as well as many of the new photographs. Because of the lapse between the time we release our book to the publishers for printing and when it actually hits the market, no doubt a lengthy addendum could be made to this chapter to cover changes to the line. Homer Laughlin has already announced its intentions of adding a new color, Chartreuse, which they plan to release by late 1997 or very early 1998. It will be Bloomingdale's exclusive for a six-month period, and the line will be limited like the Lilac. Mixing bowl sets featuring a modified version of the casserole base as the large bowl should be available by then as well, since by all reports they are ready to move into production very soon. Other possibilities are a 12½" divided Chip and Dip with a ring in the center to accept either the bouillon bowl, 5½" fruit bowl or 5½" cereal bowl for the dip; a relish tray; range-size salt and pepper shakers with handles; and a party plate with a cup ring. The five hundred millionth piece of Fiesta was produced in 1997, and the company at the time of this writing is planning a special bowl in commemoration.

The *Fiesta Collector's Quarterly* is a newsletter published by China Specialties for collectors of old and new Fiesta and features regular updates of new colors and items added to the new Fiesta line. Sample copies and subscription forms are available upon receipt of request and long SASE. The address for the newsletter is P.O. Box 471, Valley City, OH 44280. China Specialties, Inc. is an Ohio company catering to the interests of collectors of several locally produced dinnerware lines. They also publish Hall China Collector Club Newsletter and commission and distribute dated, limited edition shapes never originally made in such Hall China patterns as Autumn Leaf, Red Poppy, Silhouette, Orange Poppy, and Blue Blossom, as well as a line of Little Red Riding Hood accessories and HotOven china rolling pins. In addition, several of the special Fiesta collector items shown in this section were produced exclusively for China Specialties.

Harlequin was produced by Homer Laughlin in an effort to serve all markets and to fit every budget. It was a less expensive dinnerware and was sold without trademark through the F. W. Woolworth Company exclusively. The following is an excerpt from one of the company's original illustrated brochures:

> The new Harlequin Pottery offers a gift to table gaiety. It brings the magic of bright, exciting color to the table, dresses the festive board with pleasantness and personality, makes of every meal a cheerful and companionable occasion.
>
> The new ware comes in four lovely colors . . . Yellow, Green, Red, and Blue . . . and offers the hostess endless possibilities for creating interesting and appealing color effects on her table. All the colors are brilliant and eye-catching . . . designed to go together effectively in any combination the hostess may desire. To set a table with Harlequin is an adventure in decoration. Plates are of one color, cups of another, saucers and platters of another . . . you can give free range to your artistic instincts.
>
> And it is very easy to build up a comprehensive set of Harlequin in whatever items and colors you desire, because it may be bought by the piece at extremely reasonable prices.
>
> Sold Exclusively by
> F. W. WOOLWORTH CO. STORES

Although it was first listed on company records as early as 1936, Harlequin was not actively introduced to the public until 1938.

It was designed by Fredrick Rhead, and like Fiesta the style was pure Art Deco. Rhead again used the band of rings device as its only ornamentation, but this time chose to space the rings well away from the rim. Flat pieces were round and concave with the center areas left plain. Hollow ware pieces were cone shaped; bowls were flared. Handles were applied with small ornaments at their bases and, with few exceptions, were extremely angular.

Plate 102
Company Brochure, 1979.

Plate 102

Over the years the color assortment grew to include all of Fiesta's lovely colors with the exceptions of ivory and dark blue. The original colors (those mentioned in the brochure we just quoted), however, were developed just for Harlequin. Harlequin yellow was a lighter and brighter tint than Fiesta yellow; the green was a spruce green, and the blue tended toward a mauve shade. It is interesting to note that the color the company referred to as "red" is actually maroon. To avoid confusion, today's collectors reserve "red" for the orange-red color of Fiesta red.

It seems logical here to conclude that because Harlequin was not extensively promoted until 1938 that it would have been then or soon after that the line was expanded and new colors added. The new colors of the '40s were red (orange-red like Fiesta's — called tangerine by the company), rose (though records show a color called salmon that preceded rose, if indeed these are two individual shades, the difference is so slight it is of no significance to today's collectors), turquoise, and light green. (There are some pieces whose production dates we can't pinpoint beyond the fact that they were not part of the original line but were listed as discontinued by 1952. Many of these are rarely if ever found in light green. This leads us to believe that light green may not have been added until the mid-'40s.)

Gray, chartreuse, and forest (dark) green were new in the '50s. Harlequin yellow, turquoise, and rose continued to be produced. By 1959 the color assortment was reduced to four colors again — red (coinciding with the resumed production of Fiesta red), turquoise, Harlequin yellow, and the last new color, medium green.

The original line consisted of these items: 10", 9", 7", and 6" plates; 8" soup plate; 9" nappy; salt and pepper shakers; covered casserole; teacup and saucer; creamer, regular; sugar bowl; 11" platter; 5½" fruit; double egg cup; and 4½" tumbler.

These pieces were soon added to the original line: cream soup cup, sauce boat, after dinner cup and saucer, novelty creamer, 13" platter, teapot, syrup*, service water jug, 36s bowl, basketweave ashtray, regular ashtray, 36s oatmeal, individual salad bowl, 22-oz. jug, 4½" tumbler, ashtray saucer*, basketweave nut dish, relish tray with inserts*, individual egg cup*, individual creamer*, candle holders*, marmalade*, butter dish, large cup (tankard), and 9" baker. Of the assortment, those items marked with an asterisk (indicating them to be rare or non-existent in light green) were probably the first to be discontinued. Knowing that the Fiesta line suffered a severe pruning during 1944–'45, it would certainly follow that the same fate would befall Harlequin.

The material available to us for study dated May 1952 indicates that even more pieces had by then been dropped: the 9" baker, the covered butter dish, the individual creamer, and the tankard.

Harlequin proved to be quite popular and sold very well into the late '50s when sales began to diminish. Records show that the final piece was actually manufactured in 1964.

In 1939 the Hamilton Ross Co. offered a Harlequin look-alike which they called Sevilla. It came in assorted solid colors, eight in all, with the same angular handles, similar style and decoration. The round platter was distinctive. It featured closed handles formed by the band of rings device which was allowed to sweep gradually outward to just past mid-point; no doubt you have seen an occasional piece.

In 1979 Homer Laughlin announced that they had been approached and would comply with a request from the F.W. Woolworth Company to reissue the Harlequin line, one of that company's all time best-sellers, as part of their 100th Anniversary celebration. The Harlequin Ironstone dinnerware they produced was a very limited line and is easily recognized. It was made in two original colors: yellow and turquoise; a medium green that was slightly different than the original; and a new shade, coral. The sugar bowl was restyled with closed handles and a solid finial. A round platter (the original was oval) in coral was included in the 45-pc. set which was comprised of only plates, salad plates, cereal/soups, cups and saucers, yellow sugar, turquoise creamer, and a round green vegetable bowl. The plates were backstamped Homer Laughlin (the old ones are not marked), and even the pieces made from authentic molds are easy to distinguish from the old Harlequin. Because many of the lovely colors of the original line and virtually none of its unique accessory pieces were reproduced, this late line has never been a threat to the investments of the many collectors who love Harlequin dinnerware. We have talked with several dealers who actually felt the reissue stimulated interest in the old line.

A letter from the company dated April 1983 advised that Woolworth's as well as a few other dealers throughout the country were carrying the new Harlequin. It stated that a few round platters and vegetable bowls had been made in yellow by mistake, and that some of these were backstamped "through error in the Dipping Department." Production continued for no more than a couple of years; and compared to the old line, sales were much more limited.

Plate 103

Medium Green Harlequin.
Medium green Harlequin is even rarer than medium green Fiesta. The water pitcher is extremely rare; so is the teapot. No more than four or five of either are accounted for at this time. Only one novelty creamer is known to exist. (See Plate 112.)

Plate 104

Basketweave Ashtray (left front).
    None of the ashtrays were in the original assortment, but all were added very early — possibly even before 1940. The basketweave version may be found in all twelve colors including medium green.
Ashtray Saucer (center).
    This is an unusual item, made to serve a dual purpose. These are hard to find; and because none have been reported in the '50s colors (gray, chartreuse, and forest green for this line), medium green or light green, they were probably discontinued in the mid-'40s. Advanced collectors question the existence of rose — let us know if you have one.
Regular Ashtray.
    So dubbed by collectors to make a distinction between the three styles, this one comes in the first eight colors only; it's scarce in light green.

Plate 105

Ashtray Saucer.
    Though very rare, a few of the ashtray saucers have been reported in ivory — not a standard Harlequin color, though we know of an ivory tumbler as well.

Note: In the early 1980s, HLC produced a line of dinnerware in ivory with rusty brown speckles. The salad and dinner plates were made from Harlequin molds. A second line utilizing the speckled glaze was decorated with a textured rim band and a blooming strawberry plant in the center well.

Plate 103

Plate 104

Plate 105

Plate 106

36s Oatmeal Bowl (far left).

 Shown here in light green, the 36s oatmeal measures 6½" in diameter. They're scarce in spruce green and maroon. See the chapter entitled "Dating Codes and English Measurements" for an explanation of the term "36s."

Nappy (center back).

 The nappy, shown in spruce green, was part of the original line and can be found in all colors, although it is rare in medium green. It's 9" in diameter.

Individual Salad Bowl (right back).

 The individual salad is not so hard to find in the '50s colors; it's scarce in red, maroon, spruce green, and medium green.

36s Bowl (far right).

 Shown in a very rare color, medium green, the 36s bowl was evidently made not much later than 1959 when this color was added to the line. It's scarce in maroon and spruce.

Fruit Bowl, 5½" (center front).

 This bowl has also been found in a slightly larger version (6" diameter) in maroon, blue, spruce green, and yellow.

Plate 107

Cream Soup Bowl.

 This piece can be found in all colors; like its Fiesta counterpart, it's very rare in medium green and commands a hefty price when one comes up for sale.

Plate 108

Oval Baker.

 Discontinued before the '50s colors were introduced, the oval baker is found in the first eight colors only. (Remember, though rose was a '50s color in Fiesta, it was introduced to the Harlequin line soon after 1938.) This bowl measures 9" in length.

Plate 107

Plate 106

Plate 108

Plate 109

Mixing Bowls.

These are the Kitchen Kraft bowls — the original owner bought them from the factory by mail order for $2.05 plus postage ($1.00 for the 10", 65¢ for the 8", and 40¢ for the 6"). They are unmarked. The set was also available with the smallest bowl in red for an additional 20¢.

Plate 110

Casserole.

These are scarce in the '50s colors — especially dark green — and very rare in medium green.

Plate 111

Demitasse Coffee Cup and Saucer.

The little demitasses have become rare in the '50s colors — gray, chartreuse, and forest green — and they're extremely so in medium green. They don't appear on the 1959 listing when medium green was introduced, so they couldn't have been made in any large quantity in that color.

Large Cup.

In the past we have called the larger cup the "tankard," simply because a tankard was found listed as discontinued before 1952, and this was the only piece of Harlequin for which we didn't have a name. However as an astute Harlequin collector has pointed out, since this item has been found in only the later color assortment (chartreuse, forest green, rose, turquoise, yellow, very rarely in medium green) and not at all in the colors that were dropped early, it was obviously not discontinued before '52 and is therefore not our "tankard." But we now believe that the '50s colors were introduced in the fall of 1951, so if this were the tankard, as another collector suggests may yet be the case, the fact that it was discontinued by 1952 would explain why it is so rare. But this line of reasoning has a couple of flaws! I have one in medium green, a 1959 color, and though the handle is typically angular like Harlequin, the body of these cups is the same shape as the Epicure cups from the mid-'50s! Can anyone solve the mystery?

Plate 109

Plate 110

Plate 111

Plate 112

Novelty Creamer.

Until this edition, we've always reported that the novelty creamer was non-existent in medium green, but this photo shows there's at least one — and collectors believe this is the only one! It's shown alongside another very rare item, a medium green service water pitcher.

Plate 113

Butter Dish, ½-lb.

Originally a Jade/Century piece, this butter dish was later glazed in Harlequin and Riviera colors and sold with both lines. They have been found in these colors: cobalt blue, rose, mauve blue, spruce green, light green, maroon, turquoise, red, ivory, and Fiesta and Harlequin yellows.

Plate 114

Candle Holders.

These are not at all easy to find in any color, in fact, we once thought they were non-existent in light green. But at some point in time, someone reported that they had a pair of light green ones in their collection. Today's advanced Harlequin buffs question this report, since in their networkings they have never encountered any of these in light green. Can someone out there shed some light on this?

Plate 115

High-Lip Creamer (top row).

The "high-lip" creamer is found in the four original colors only. Note the difference in the length of the lips on the two shown. The fact that they were trimmed by hand doesn't wholly explain the difference, since only these two variations have been reported. Evidently the style was deliberately changed at some point.

Individual Creamer (top right).

You'll find this tiny pitcher only in the first eight colors. They're really not at all difficult to find, but they are scarce in light green.

Regular Creamer (bottom row).

This item is available in all twelve colors.

Sugar Bowl.

One collector reports that upon comparing several sugar bowls in his collection, he suspects those with the inside rings were earlier and that these rings were eliminated sometime during the '40s.

Novelty Creamer.

As far as we know, only one of these exists in medium green, but you can expect to find them in all the other colors.

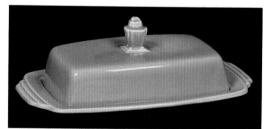

Plate 113

Plate 112

Plate 114

Plate 116

Salt and Pepper Shakers.

These were made in all of Harlequin's colors; they're all easy to find except medium green.

Jug, 22-oz.

These are commonly found in the first eleven colors; they're extremely rare in medium green — only three have been reported.

Deep Plate.

These can be found in all twelve colors; they're 8" in diameter.

Sauce Boat.

These are fairly easy to find in any of the twelve Harlequin colors, though they're scarce in medium green.

Plate 115

Plate 116

Plate 117

Japanese Imports.

The basketweave ashtray and nut dish were copied from these Japanese imports. We thought you'd enjoy seeing the originals. They carry the mark "Marutomo Ware Made in Japan."

Plate 118

Marmalade.

Found in the first eight colors only, they're scarce in rose, and light green marmalades are very rare.

Nut Dish.

The small basketweave nut dishes are found in the first eight colors; they're scarce in light green, though not as rare as we once believed.

Individual Egg Cup.

Though fairly common in yellow, spruce green, mauve blue, maroon, turquoise, rose, and red, they're very rare in light green.

Double Egg Cup.

This egg cup will hold an egg in both the top and bottom (not all at once!) The small end was to accommodate a boiled egg; the larger end was for a poached egg, the custom at that time being to dunk toast points into the soft poached egg yolk. They're found in all twelve colors, but only four have been reported in medium green.

Perfume Bottle.

These are not a standard part of the Harlequin line but are of interest to Harlequin collectors since they were dipped in Harlequin glazes. They're hard to find; most of them are yellow, but light green has also been reported.

Plate 117

Plate 119

Tumblers.

These were discontinued before the '50s colors were introduced, so they're found in only the first eight colors. Remember, though rose was strictly a '50s color in the Fiesta line, it was made in Harlequin from the late '30s until late in the '50s, so don't be surprised to find a rose example, even though we don't show one here. One has been reported in ivory, a non-standard Harlequin color.

Service Water Pitcher.

Look for the Fiesta-like band of rings near the base of this pitcher. This will help you identify the Harlequin pitcher from several look-alikes by other companies. These were produced in all twelve colors; they're very rare in medium green and scarce in gray and dark green. Several have now been reported in Fiesta yellow; we once saw one of these etched "Treasure Island, 1939."

Plate 118

Plate 119

Plate 120

Plates, 10", 9", 7", 6".

  The 10" dinner plate is becoming very hard to find; the 9" and 7" have been reported in ivory, not a standard Harlequin color.

Platters, 10", 13".

  These are generally easy to find in all twelve colors, though they're both rare in medium green.

Plate 121

Relish Tray.

  These are rare! As strange as it seems, the true Harlequin relish tray base is found only in turquoise; these pie-wedge inserts are occasionally found in bases of another color, but those bases are actually Fiesta. The inserts are found in only six of the first eight colors — no light green or spruce. The color combination as shown is the most common, but other combinations have also been reported. Two examples with all rose inserts have been found.

Plate 122

Syrup.

  Syrups are scarce and have been reported in only red, yellow, mauve blue, spruce green, turquoise, light green, and ivory — and just one in each of the last three colors. (Let us hear from you if you have one in those colors.) They're most often found in red and yellow. Harlequin syrups are much rarer than their Fiesta counterparts.

Plate 123

Teacups and Saucers.

  These are relatively easy to find in all twelve colors. One has been found in a non-standard shade, Skytone blue.

Teapot.

  Teapots were made in all twelve colors but are very rare in medium green.

Plate 120

Plate 121

Plate 122

Plate 123

Harlequin Animals

During the late '30s and early '40s when miniatures such as these were enjoying a hey-day, HLC produced this menagerie as a part of the Harlequin line. There are six, each produced in four colors: maroon, spruce green, mauve blue, and yellow. They were marketed primarily through Woolworth Company stores.

There are no original Harlequin Animals other than those pictured in Plate 124, although you may find some that are very similar. The duck has a twin, a perpetually hungry little gander — his head bent into a permanent feeding position; but he was made by the Brush Pottery Company. Although several collectors were almost sure their 2½" elephant belonged in the group, HLC disowned him. A donkey look-alike pulling a cart may make you wonder at first, but a closer examination will reveal an uncharacteristic lack of sharp detail, and some of these have been found to bear a "California" mark.

"Maverick" animals is a term adopted by collectors to indicate animals that have been glazed by someone outside the Homer Laughlin China Company. In rare cases, you may find one in a standard Harlequin color that has been completely covered with gold, or it may be simply gold trimmed. One company involved in decorating the animals was Kaulware of Chicago, who utilized an iridescent glaze and gold hand-painted trim. You will find salt and pepper shakers in a slightly smaller size, indicating that they were cast from molds made from the original animals (See Plate 126). The Maverick guard cats in Plate 127 are in white with colored trim.

Another company responsible for producing some of the Mavericks was founded by John Kass, who operated in the East Liverpool, Ohio, area. During the Depression after his retail business failed, Kass built a small pottery, employed members of his family, and began to make novelty items — salt and pepper shakers, small animal figures (Mavericks among them), and cups and saucers. A descendant of Kass's explained that it was a common practice in those days for area potters to "make each other's items, and no one took offense." All Kass's work was done painstakingly by hand from the casting to the final decoration. Business increased in the 1940s; the old buildings were replaced with modern structures, and more people were employed. "We made the Harlequin animals from the very beginning," she continues. "For some reason the ducks and penguins were made right up into the 1950s." The letter goes on to say that there were other companies in the area who also made these animals. You will find that some of these are considerably smaller than the Harlequin animals and made of a finer, more porcelain-like material. Though most will be white with gold trim, some may be in colors. We have a gold-trimmed cobalt cat; and, until you compare it with the genuine article, you can't be sure that it isn't authentic. It measures 2½" long compared to the one I have in maroon that is a good ¼" longer. These smaller animals are worth considerably less than Mavericks that are full size or nearly so.

Plate 124
Original Harlequin Animals in Authentic Glazes.

Plate 125
"Maverick Animals."

Plate 126
Salt and Pepper Shakers.
These penguins are a slightly smaller size, indicating that they were cast from molds made from the original animals.

Plate 127
"Maverick Guard Cats."

Plate 128
Red Animals.
Though probably not a production run, there are a few red cats being found; a red duck and penguin have been reported as well as a penguin in black. Be alert for painted frauds. Collectors tell us of finding red animals whose color, feel, and weight were perfect but the paint was chipping off.

Plate 129
Rare Animals.
Shown are turquoise, light green, and cobalt blue animals borrowed from HLC for their portrait photo. These are from their archives — don't expect to find them on the market.

Plate 124

Plate 125

Plate 126

Plate 127

Plate 128

Plate 129

Riviera and Ivory Century

Riviera was introduced by HCL in 1938 and was sold exclusively by the Murphy Company. In contrast to Fiesta and Harlequin, the line was quite limited. It was unmarked, lighter in weight, and therefore less expensive. Only rarely will you find a piece with the Homer Laughlin gold stamp. Of the three colored dinnerware lines, it has the rather dubious distinction of being the only one which was not originally created as such. Its forerunner was a line called Century — an ivory line with a vellum glaze. Century shapes were also decorated with a wide variety of decals and were the bases of many lines such as Mexicana and Hacienda. An enterprising designer (Rhead, no doubt) applied the popular colored glazes to these shapes, and Riviera was born. Even the shakers were from another line. They were originally designed as Tango, which accounts for the six-section design in contrast to the square Riviera shape.

Riviera is in very short supply; and much to the chagrin of Riviera collectors everywhere, mint condition pieces are very few indeed. Flat pieces were especially bad to chip — plates, platters, saucers, and undersides of lids; but when it is found with no chips, the glaze is nearly always in beautiful condition.

Colors are mauve blue, red, yellow, light green, and ivory. On rare occasions, dark blue pieces are found, evidently made for special color effects. Ivory pieces are technically Century (the old price lists we've seen never show but four colors), and you will find a more diversified assortment in ivory than in the colored glazes. However, collectors appreciate the effect of the ivory with their Riviera and value these items as worthwhile additions to their collections.

Records for this line are especially scanty; but as accurately and completely as possible, here is a listing of the items in the line as it was first introduced. Sizes have been translated from the English measurements listed by the company and in our previous editions to actual sizes to the nearest inch.

11" Dish (Platter)	13" Dish (Platter)	10" Plate	9" Plate
6" Plate	Teacup and Saucer	Fruit	9" Baker (Oval Vegetable Bowl)
Salt and Pepper Shakers	Covered Casserole	8" Deep Plate	8" Nappy
6" Oatmeal	Tumbler (with Handle)	Open Jug	Teapot
Sauce Boat	Creamer	(Also Found with Lid)	Covered Sugar

We have also found 15" platters, a covered syrup pitcher, and two sizes of butter dishes — a half-pound and a quarter-pound. In addition, there is a juice set. The juice jugs are standard though scarce in yellow, unusual in red, and extremely rare in mauve blue.

Although it is uncertain just when Riviera was discontinued, it was sometime prior to 1950. Riviera is a challenge to collect, but you can be sure the effort will be worthwhile — it's a very attractive line as you'll see in the following color plates!

Plate 130
Syrup, Demitasse Cup and Saucer, Fast-Stand Sauce Dish.
   The syrup is very rare in ivory, as are all the items in this photograph. We saw a fast-stand sauce dish on our visit to the morgue and for years thought it was strictly experimental, but since then four or five have been discovered.

Plate 130

Plate 131

Cream Soup Bowl With Liner.

Don't expect to find these in the colored glazes — they're technically Century, but collectors enjoy adding them to their set of Riviera. Egg cups and 8" plates may also be found but only in ivory. Several ivory pieces have been reported with gold or silver bands. You'll see an example of some on page 93.

Plate 132

Tidbit Tray, 4½" Jug, Utility Bowl, Salt and Pepper Shakers.

Here are more Century items. You will find the shakers in Riviera colors, and one two-tier tidbit tray has been reported in mauve blue. But the jug (a size between the batter pitcher and the syrup) and the utility bowl were never part of the Riviera line. One collector reports the earliest backstamp she has in her Century collection indicates a 1933 production date.

Plate 131

Plate 132

Plate 133

Butter Dish.

    This green example still has the original Riviera sticker and price tag! (See also Plate 137).

Plate 134

Butter Dishes.

    These ¼-lb. butter dishes are shown here in turquoise and cobalt, colors rarely seen on this item. (See also Plate 137).

Plate 135

Covered Jugs.

    These are quite hard to find. (See also Plate 137).

Plate 136

Bowls: Baker, Nappy, Fruit, Oatmeal.

    Left to right: Baker, oval with straight sides, 9" long; Nappy, 7¼" diameter; Baker, oval with curved sides, 9" long. In front: Fruit, 5½"; Oatmeal, 6". The oatmeal is slightly deeper than the fruit bowl and is rather scarce.

Plate 137

Butter Dishes, Creamer and Sugar Bowl, Covered Jug.

    As far as we know, the mauve blue and the yellow covered jugs have never been found with a lid. Have you seen one? The larger ½-lb. butter dish is more readily found than the smaller and is available in mauve blue, rose, spruce green, light green, turquoise, maroon, cobalt blue, red, ivory, and in both Fiesta and Harlequin yellow. The ¼-lb. size is rare in turquoise and cobalt. For further information on the butter dish, see the section on Jade.

Plate 133

Plate 134

Plate 135

Plate 136

Plate 137

Plate 138

Casserole.

A very nice piece and one that may prove difficult to find; the large size of these casseroles along with their distinctive styling and wonderful colors make them spectacular additions to any Riviera collection.

Plate 139

Sauce Boat.

These have never been considered at all hard to find, but since sending out our last survey, we have had many comments made to us indicating that Riviera in general is becoming scarce.

Plates 140 – 144

Batter Sets.

Complete with tray in cobalt, covered syrup pitcher in red, and tall covered jug in green (used for mixing, storing, and pouring pancake and waffle batter), these sets are quite unique since they utilize one of the rare cobalt blue pieces and the cover for the tall jug. This is the standard color combination for these sets. Until we received the photo in Plate 141, a very unusual set glazed entirely in red, the jug complete with the lid had been reported in only green and ivory. Occasionally you may see a set in ivory either with floral or scrollwork decals similar to those shown in Plates 142 and 144, but these are rare. Two factors make the set in Plate 143 different from the others: the covered sugar bowl, which is a seldom-seen component, and the very rare 11½" square platter. These pieces are stamped with the Wells peacock mark and "Warranted 18 Carat Gold."

Plate 138

Plate 139

Plate 140

Plate 141

Plate 142

Plate 143

Plate 144

Plates 145 – 146

Sugar and Creamer Sets.

  Here are two unique sets — one in light green with gold trim and one in a most unusual lime green.

Plate 147

Teapot, Teacups and Saucers.

  Teapots have been scarce for several years. Now that Riviera is getting harder and harder to find, good serving pieces are all in short supply. Even the once-common cups and saucers are difficult to acquire in mint condition.

Plate 148

Juice Pitcher, Juice Tumblers.

  The pitcher is scarce in any color but is standard in yellow. It's very rare in mauve blue, shown here, and red (see Plate 149). In the original sets, the tumblers were turquoise, mauve blue, red, yellow, light green, and ivory.

Plate 145

Plate 146

Plate 147

Plate 148

Plate 149

Juice Pitcher.

Shown here in the very rare red color.

Plate 150

Compartment Plate, 9¾".

This unique item was reported to us just as we went to press with the Seventh Edition, and to date, we've never heard of a second one. It was a gift to a collector given by a friend with the comment, "This looks like that stuff you collect."

Plate 151

Salt and Pepper Shakers, Syrup Pitcher, Deep Plate, Handled Tumblers.

As you can see, there are six orange-like segments that make up the design of the salt and pepper shakers. These were borrowed from the Tango line, so you may find them in Tango's color too. Two pairs have been found in a true primary red glaze — origin unconfirmed. Here's the covered syrup in red again; it's a darling piece and very hard to find. Ivory tumblers are scarce and command high prices. Though not a Homer Laughlin product, you may find sets of glass tumblers (one style with a smooth surface, another with vertically paneled sides), each with a solid band of one of the Riviera colors at the rim. One set was bought at auction still in the original box marked "Juanita Beverage Set, Rosenthal and Ruben, Inc., Binghampton, NY, 1938." There were two each of the four colors (light green, mauve blue, yellow, and red) in four sizes: 3", 3½", 4", and 5¼". Matching swizzle sticks completed the forty-piece set. See the chapter titled "Go-Alongs" for more information.

Plate 152

Plates, 10", 9", 7", 6".

The 10" plates are very hard to find. The 7" plate is sometimes found in cobalt blue, and collectors also report this size in Fiesta yellow. Perhaps, as one reader suggests, they were dipped in these colors to go with a Riviera/Fiesta ensemble such as in the ad in the chapter on advertising ephemera.

Plate 153

Platters.

Shown: 11½", no handles; 11¼" with closed handles. You'll also find 13¼" and 12" platters with the closed handles, and one in ivory measuring 16" has been reported as well. There is a square platter with handles that measures 11½"; it's shown with the batter set in Plate 143.

Plate 149

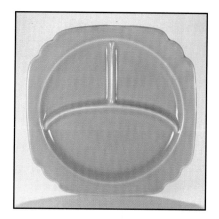

Plate 150

Plate 151

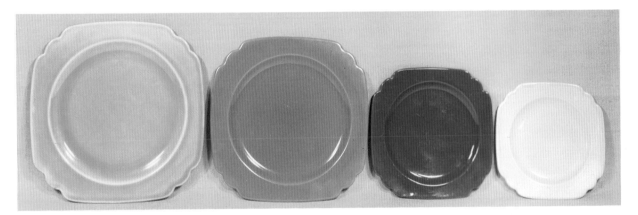

Plate 152

Plate 153

Amberstone

This "brown Fiesta" seems to have generated lots of enthusiasm among collectors; and it's easy to see why — especially when some of the hollow ware pieces are found with the familiar Fiesta cast-indented trademark!

Amberstone was introduced in 1967, three years before the Fiesta line was restyled; yet the illustration on an old order blank shows that the sugar and creamer, cup, teapot, soup/cereal, casserole, and coffee server were from the same molds that were later used for Fiesta Ironstone. Only on the pieces that had relatively flat areas large enough to permit decoration do you find the black, machine-stamped underglaze pattern. The remainder were simply solid brown.

Sold under the trade name of Genuine Sheffield dinnerware, it was produced by HLC exclusively for supermarket promotions; and several large grocery store chains featured Amberstone as a premium. (For a listing of items offered, see "Suggested Values" in back of book.)

Plate 154
Amberstone Setting.

Plate 154

Plates 155 – 158

Additional Amberstone Shapes.

The marmalade is shown in Plate 158, and the mustard (alongside salt and pepper shakers for size comparison) is in Plate 157. Note the Ironstone pieces: casserole, flared fruit bowl, and sauce boat stand. Even though there was no butter dish listed in the Ironstone assortment (nor in the older Fiesta line), here's one in Amberstone, and there was one in the Casualstone line as well. Collectors question the existence of the Amberstone mug, but one was listed on an old company brochure and included in the line drawing on the other side. They have straight sides and — believe it or not — a Fiesta ring handle. Let us know if you've ever seen one! We also have a report of an Amberstone brown cup with an old Fiesta handle and another on a Nautilus shape.

Plate 155

Plate 156

Plate 157

Plate 158

Casualstone

In 1970 Homer Laughlin produced a second line of dinnerware to be sold exclusively through supermarket promotions. This dinnerware was called Casualstone and was presented under the trade name "Coventry." The Antique Gold of the Fiesta Ironstone was decorated with an intricate gold machine-stamped design; which, like Amberstone, appeared on only the shallow items. An old order blank shows that it was less expensive than the Amberstone of three years previous, possibly because a color already in production was used. (For a listing of available items, see "Suggested Values" in back of book.)

Plate 159

Carnival

Carnival was made exclusively for the Quaker Oats Company who gave it away to their customers, one piece packed in each box of Mother's Carnival Oats. While no records exist to verify the year in which it was first produced, we must assume it was in the late '30s or early '40s by reason of the color assortment. Harlequin yellow, turquoise (both of which were first used by HLC in 1938), light green, and Fiesta red were evidently the original colors. The only mention of Carnival in company files was dated 1952; it lists these glazes: dark green, turquoise, gray, and Harlequin yellow. You'll also occasionally find examples in cobalt and ivory — notice the cups on the front of the box shown below. (The 1952 record also itemized the pieces in production at that time; these are listed with suggested values in the back of the book.) A company representative recalled that coupons were included in the boxes, redeemable for the larger pieces. Perhaps there were plates, bowls, and platters — to date, however, none have been found, leading collectors to believe it was a breakfast set shown in its entirety on the box.

Plates 160 – 161
Examples of Carnival.

Plate 160

Plate 161

Epicure is a '50s line — with the '50s streamline styling and pastel colors. Anyone who remembers what a great era that was for growing up can tell you about pink and gray. Argyle socks were pink and gray! If your sweater was pink, your skirt or corduroys were gray. Turquoise was popular in home decorating — even down to appliances. And these were the colors of Epicure: Dawn Pink, Charcoal Gray, Turquoise Blue, and Snow White.

The designer was Don Schreckengost, who also designed Rhythm. We can find no information pinpointing production dates, but collectors tell us that virtually all of their Epicure is stamped 1955. The only exception ever reported was a set of plates in pink that were marked 1960. The line consisted of the following items:

Bowls: Cereal/Soup
      Fruit
      Nappy, 8"
      Nappy, 9"
Platter, Large Oval
Salt and Pepper Shakers
Sugar Bowl with Lid
Teacup and Saucer
2-Tier Tidbit Tray
Casseroles: Covered Vegetable, Individual

Coffeepot, 10"
Creamer
Gravy Bowl
Ladle, 5½"
Nut Dish
Pickle (Small Oval Platter)
Plates: Dessert, 6½"
      Snack, 8½"
      Dinner, 10"

The nut dish could pass for a butter pat; and one collector tells us that of the eleven in his collection, all are turquoise. In fact, no other colors have ever been reported. Have you ever seen an ashtray in this line? We've heard only rumors — as far as we know, none exists.

Epicure is not easy to find, but many collectors view it as an exciting challenge. Dealers tell us that it sells well due to its famous designer and today's strong interest in the designs and colors of the '50s.

Plate 162
Tidbit, Creamer, Cereal/Soup, Sugar Bowl, Salt Shaker, Cup and Saucer, Individual Casserole.
    Very nearly the same size as the sugar bowl, the individual casserole (shown in Charcoal Gray) is very hard to find. Collectors tell us the cups and saucers are also very scarce, and one says he has a Fiesta cup in Epicure charcoal gray.

Plate 163
Coffeepot, Plates, Nappy, Gravy Bowl, Ladle, Covered Vegetable Casserole.
    The pink nappy is the 9" size (it actually measures 8¾"); plates are 10" and 6½". The turquoise gravy boat holds a charcoal gray ladle.

Plate 162

Plate 163

Jubilee

Jubilee was presented by Homer Laughlin in 1948 in celebration of their 75th year of ceramic leadership. Shapes were simple and contemporary. It was offered in four colors: Celadon Green (blue-gray), Shell Pink, Mist Gray, and Cream Beige. Very soon after its introduction, HLC introduced many other lines of dinnerware employing its basic shapes.

Plate 164
Double Egg Cup; Coupe Soup, 8"; Demitasse Cup and Saucer; Plates, 6", 7", 9", 10"; Teacup and Saucer; Cereal/Soup Bowl, 6"; Fruit Bowl, 5½".

Plate 165
Platters, 11", 13"; Teapot, Coffeepot, Creamer and Sugar Bowl, Casserole; Nappy, 8½"; Salt and Pepper Shakers; Fast-Stand Sauce Boat; Chop Plate, 15".

Plate 164

Plate 165

Plate 166

The Jubilee Pamphlet.
  Old company price lists, especially for lines other than Fiesta, are very scarce. They're a wonderful source of information, and collectors pay dearly for them.

Plate 166

Plate 167

Kitchen Kraft Bowl Set.

This set was glazed in the Jubilee colors and along with the Fiesta juice set shown in Plate 33 was part of a promotion to stimulate sales of the Jubilee line. All of these items are very rare, and because of that, it's taken us what seems like an unbelievably long time to arrive at correct conclusions. Fact: only one of these three bowls was ever produced in gray, and that is the 10" size. As far as we know, only one of these has ever been found. The colors do not vary from size to size; they are as shown — Shell Pink 6", Celadon Green 8", and Mist Gray 10" — and the gray matches Fiesta gray exactly.

Plate 167

Skytone

This is a seldom-seen but very attractive line of dinnerware utilizing the shapes of Jubilee. It was sold through the '50s in both the plain blue and white seen here and with decals. What makes this line unusual is that the beautiful blue hue comes not from the glaze but from the clay used in its production. In addition to the pieces shown with the Jubilee line, you may also find a butter dish in the Amberstone shape with a blue lid and a white base.

Plate 168

Example of Skytone.

Plate 168

Suntone

Here's another colored line of dinnerware — the shapes are Jubilee, and it is from the same time period as Skytone. The clay used in its production was terra-cotta brown, the glaze itself was clear. According to company records, decaled Suntone was marketed as well. The Jubilee shapes proved very popular through the '50s, and the company utilized them for many attractive patterns, changing the name of the shape to Debutante when the lines were white-glazed.

Plate 169
Cup and Saucer.
   A very interesting, very small cup and saucer, shown with the teacup and Jubilee demitasse cup for comparison. Was it from a child's set? We don't know. Does anyone?

Plate 170
Example of Suntone Setting.

Plate 169

Plate 170

Pastel Nautilus

HLC's Nautilus was made from the '30s into the '50s. It was often decaled; it was fancy-trimmed without decals; it was combined with Fiesta's first four colors to make the four "Harmony" sets; and in 1940 (no other date marks have been reported) it was dipped in the pastel glazes of Serenade — pink, yellow, green, and blue — and offered to the public as Pastel Nautilus.

The line is scarce, to be sure, but very attractive; and if you have the patience to work at it, a complete set would represent quite an accomplishment. For a complete listing of available items, see "Suggested Values" in the back of the book. Note: Advanced collectors question the existence of the after-dinner cup and saucer. Can you verify?

Plate 171
9", 7", and 6" Plates; Teacup; Double Egg Cup; and Creamer.

Plate 172
Casserole.

Plate 173
Bowls.
   Clockwise: tab-handled soup, 6" cereal, 5" fruit, and cream soup.

Plate 171   Photo by Shel Izen

Plate 172   Photo by Shel Izen

Plate 173   Photo by Shel Izen

Rhythm

With Rhythm steadily emerging from its "sleeper" state, more accurate information than we had in the beginning is being pieced together by its dedicated fans. Those with large collections report backstamps with dates indicating a span of production from 1950 to 1960. It was made in Harlequin yellow, chartreuse, gray, forest green, and burgundy (collectors call it maroon).

Rhythm shapes are simple and streamlined with a "designer" look. Don Schreckengost was that designer, who early in 1982 was interviewed by a newsletter which was at that time being published in the East. In that interview, Mr. Schreckengost revealed that the spoon rest which we thought to be Harlequin was, in fact, a piece he had originated for the Rhythm line.

Several lines featuring decals on a white glaze were manufactured during the '50s utilizing Rhythm shapes. You will find several examples of these in the color plates. The spoon rests are often found with decals — Rhythm Rose and American Provincial are the most common. (For a complete listing of available items, see "Suggested Values" in the back of the book.)

Plate 174
Casserole, Nappy, Soup, Fruit, Footed Cereal/Chowder.
The 5½" fruit is shown center front; to the right is the 5½" footed cereal. The nappy (forest green) measures 9"; the soup is 8¼". The casserole is very hard to find.

Plate 174

Plate 175

Plate, 8"; Sauce Boat, Soup/Cereal Bowls.

The 8" yellow plate and the brown soup/cereal are marked Rhythm though both are non-standard colors. The sauce boat shown here in cobalt has also been found in black, turquoise, and brown, made in these colors to go with other lines. It was a common practice to mix hollow ware shapes from one line with flatware shapes from another to create new patterns of dinnerware. Cavalier and Charm House were from the same period as Rhythm, and all three shapes were often blended.

Plate 176

Calendar Plate.

The company issued a calendar plate for a number of years, using whatever blanks were available. This one is Rhythm.

Plate 177

Mixing Bowls.

These are the Kitchen Kraft bowls; this particular combination of color identifies them as Rhythm. They measure 10" (always chartreuse), 8" (yellow), and 6" (forest green), and they have a dry (wiped free of glaze) foot. They were part of a sales campaign, a ploy the company also used to promote Fiesta and Jubilee. Possibly the most exciting news in the Eighth Edition is the discovery of a maroon Fiesta juice tumbler, which seems to be the clincher to the theory that the gray juice pitcher and tumblers in chartreuse, forest green, and gray were a Rhythm promotion. (See Plate 32 for more information.)

Plate 175

Plate 176

Plate 177

Plate 178
Plates, Sauce Boat and Stand, Sugar Bowl, Snack Plate, Salt and Pepper Shakers.
   Plates measure 10", 9", 7", and 6"; the 7" and 8" (see Plate 175) are scarce. Though once considered nonexistent, we have had reports of a few divided plates in maroon. They're very scarce in any color.

Plate 179
Spoon Rests.
   These have been reported in yellow, turquoise, and forest green, as well as a very rare example in medium green. One in turquoise was found with a Harlequin label still intact, so obviously these were sold with that line as well. You'll also see them in white with a decal decoration, but those are much less valuable.

Plate 178

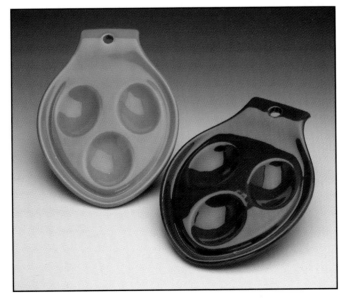

Plate 179

Plate 180

Three-Tier Tidbit, Platters, Cup and Saucer, Teapot.
    These platters measure 13½" and 11½" long. We've had a report that a Rhythm platter has been found with the turkey decal.

Plate 181

Demitasse Cups.
    These utilize a standard HLC dinnerware shape called Brittany. They're shown along with a sugar bowl for scale.

Plate 180

Plate 181

Plate 182

The focus of this photograph is the salad bowl (shown with other pieces for scale). Collectors report that these are often acquired from among the remnants of original Rhythm sets. They've been found in forest green as well as turquoise. If you have information concerning these bowls, let us hear from you.

Plate 183

These flat soup bowls are Brittany shapes glazed in all the Rhythm colors. They're marked HLC and carry dates coinciding with Rhythm's production period.

Plate 182

Plate 183

Serenade

Serenade was a pastel dinnerware line that was produced for only three or four years from about 1939 (it was mentioned in the American Potter's brochure from the World's Fair) until the early '40s. It was offered in four lovely pastel shades — yellow, green, pink, and blue. Although not well accepted by the public when it was introduced, today's collectors find its soft delicate hues and dainty contours appealing. There is growing interest in this elusive pattern, but prices are still relatively moderate.

Lug soups and teapots are rare; so are 10" plates. You may also find deep plates, 7" plates, 5" fruits, and 9" nappies to be scarce. Sugar bowls are harder to find than creamers, and the lid for the casserole (the only Kitchen Kraft piece dipped in Serenade colors) is very rare — only five have ever been reported.

Plate 184
Chop Plate, 13"; Teapot; Creamer and Sugar Bowl; Cup and Saucer.

Plate 184

Photo by Shel Izen

Plate 185

Casserole.

This is the standard Serenade casserole.

Plate 186

Deep Plate; Nappy, 9"; Sauce Boat; Fruit Bowl, 6"; Lug (Tab-Handled) Soup Bowl.

Plate 187

Casserole, Kitchen Kraft.

For many years, the lid to this casserole could not be found. Finally we're up to five — two in yellow, one in blue, one in ivory, and this one in green.

Plate 188

Plates, 10", 9", 6"; Platter, 12½"; Pickle Dish; Salt and Pepper Shakers.

Plate 185

Plate 186

Plate 187

Photo by Shel Izen

Photo by Shel Izen

Plate 188

Photo by Shel Izen

Tango

Tango was introduced in the late 1930s, made for promotion through Newberry's and the McLellan Stores Company, N.Y. City. For some reason, it was not a good seller — perhaps its rather Colonial design seemed a bit out of step alongside other styles of colored dinnerware. Standard colors were spruce green, mauve blue, yellow, and maroon; but, as you can see in the color plate, a few pieces may also be found in Fiesta red.

The line was rather limited; all available items are shown below, although unconfirmed rumors occasionally circulate concerning the existence of an egg cup. Until the egg cup can be verified, we assume that the line consisted of a fruit bowl; deep plate; oval vegetable bowl; round nappy; casserole with lid; creamer and sugar bowl; cup and saucer; plates, 10", 9", 7", and 6"; platter; and salt and pepper shakers. The shakers should look very familiar to Riviera collectors. They were original with this line; but since their shape was compatible, they were borrowed for use with Riviera.

Proving once again that value is a relative thing, our price survey (which represents a cross-section) indicated prices for Tango hadn't elevated any more than 10%, though the casserole had appreciated considerably. But the dyed-in-the-wool dedicated Tango collectors tell us that to them, their collections are worth much more than suggested "book" prices, because it is so scarce. And, we are sure, this is the sentiment of collectors of other minor lines as well.

The W.S. George Company made a line very similar to Tango, but their glazes are rather dull and the definition of the "petals" somewhat indistinct in comparison. You'll be able to recognize Tango by the raised line just inside the shaped rim.

Plate 189
Tango Setting.

Plate 189

Photo © Adam Anik

Wells Art Glaze

This line was produced from 1930 until at least 1935 in the colors shown, rust, peach, green, and yellow. A burnt orange matt similar to Fiesta red has also been reported as well as turquoise matt. It's a lovely design, and records list an extensive assortment. It's very scarce and to reassemble a set is a challenge, but one collectors don't mind rising to meet, and values that were for a long time stable have appreciated considerably for this edition — 25% to 30% on the average. Dealers tell us Arts and Crafts enthusiasts have discovered this line, accounting for some of the price increases. One finds his clientele prefers green, then rust above the other colors, but another considers yellow to be the bestseller. The casserole is extremely rare. (For a complete listing of available items, see "Suggested Values" in the back of the book.)

Plate 190
Chop Plate, Covered Jug, Baker, Sugar Bowl With Lid, Teacup and Saucer, Demitasse Cup and Saucer, Handled Coffee Cup.
　　The handled chop plate is 10", the covered jug is 9", and the oval baker is 9" long. The cup on the far right is inscribed "Coffee" and is 4¾" tall.

Plate 191
Teapots.
　　The teapot on the left is very scarce; only a few have been reported. Besides this one in yellow, we know of one in green and another in turquoise. Both are marked "Wells." The shape is from a standard HLC line called Empress. On the right is the traditional Wells Art Glaze teapot; you'll see it again in Plate 194.

Plate 190

Plate 191

Plate 192
Cream Soup Bowl With Underliner.
These are seldom seen items; the underliner has a recessed ring.

Plate 193
Coffee Mug.
Here's a better view of the 4¾" coffee mug, a seldom seen piece.

Plate 194
Plates, Teapot, Teacup and Saucer, Creamer and Sugar Bowl.
Shown are the 9", 8", and 6" plates, and a square one that measures 8".

Plate 192

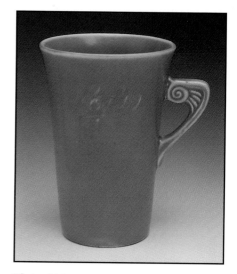

Plate 193

Plate 194

Plate 195
Covered Muffin.
   These are wonderful items and very rare. They fit on the 8" plate.

Plate 196
Batter Set.
   The covered jug, covered syrup pitcher, and oval tray comprise this very rare set. You may also find these in white with floral decals.

Plate 197
Demitasse Pot, Individual Sugar and Creamer.
   Note the differences in the handles on the sugar bowl shown here and the one in Plate 194.

Plate 195

Plate 196

Plate 197

Orange Tree Bowls

Though we've always referred to these as the "orange tree" bowls because of their resemblance to Fenton's carnival glass pattern of the same name, some collectors call the design "peach tree." Whatever you choose to call them, they're scarce — especially the small bowl. We suspect these were designed by Rhead due to the stylized tree motif very similar to designs he used earlier in his career. They range in size from 5" to 10", and though they're more common in turquoise, they've also been found in ivory, yellow, and pumpkin. On rare occasions the ivory is decorated with stripes. In addition to the one shown here with a red stripe, we've also heard from a collector who tells us that his has three green stripes — one inside the rim, one outside the rim, and one on top.

Plate 198 – 199
Orange Tree Bowls.

Plate 198

Plate 199

Five-Petal Daisy

Here's another line for those of you who enjoy a challenge. The name isn't official, merely descriptive. The official company name for this shape is "Marigold," and it was used as a basis for several decaled lines. This piece is backstamped 1937, so it was made early in the days of HLC's campaign to promote this type of colored dinnerware. This is the deep plate in the company's standard light green glaze.

Plate 200

Mexicana

When first introduced in the late '30s, Homer Laughlin's Mexican-style dinnerware lines were met with great enthusiasm. Speaking of Mexicana, which would prove to be one of their bestsellers, a tradepaper from May 1938, had this to say:

> When this Homer Laughlin pattern was first exhibited last (1937) July at the House Furnishing Show, it was an immediate smash hit. Its popularity has grown steadily ever since, and retailers have found it a constant and dependable source of profit. It started the vogue for the Mexican motif in crockery decoration which has since swept the country.
> And small wonder! For this Mexicana pattern is smart, colorful, and attractive. It embodies the old-world atmosphere of Mexico with the modern verve and personality which is so appealing to American housewives. Applied to the pleasing, beautifully designed Homer Laughlin shapes, it presents a bestseller of the first order.

Several other companies produced similarly decorated lines with a decided Mexican flavor — Paden City, Vernon Kilns, Crown, and Stetson to name but a few. Besides the Mexican lines shown in the color plates, HLC also made Arizona, decorated with a large green cactus, adobe house, yucca plant, and pottery jug; however, this line is seldom seen.

HLC's three principal Mexican decals are Mexicana, Hacienda, and Conchita. (You'll sometimes find pieces marked "Mexicana" with a gold backstamp). With the exception of a line of Hacienda on Nautilus (Plates 214 and

Plate 201A

215), these lines are virtually always found on two shapes: Century and Swing. (But a collector/dealer–friend displayed an unusual Mexicana plate at the '97 APEC Show; the shape was Liberty — see Plate 201A.) Century, based on the number of pieces that have turned up, was the much more successful line, but there are some rare items in Swing that are equally as rare and may in fact be nonexistent in Century. For example, the only demitasse cups we've heard of are on the Swing shape; they're shown in Plate 201B (in Mexicana and Hacienda), alongside a Swing teacup and saucer (in Conchita).

Neither Hacienda nor Conchita has been found with trim lines other than red, but Mexicana turns up comparatively often with blue trim — especially in Kitchen Kraft, Eggshell Nautilus, and Swing. In its first year of Century production, green and yellow trim lines were used as well. Yet here's an anomaly: the non-red trim on Century Mexicana has been reported on 10" plates, 7" plates, cups, fruits, flat soups, and serving nappies, but on no other items — not even saucers, which seems especially strange. One collector found a mixed set of cobalt Fiesta (saucers, 6" plates, sugar bowl and original creamer) with blue-line Mexicana (cups, 10" plates, and flat soups). The Mexicana cup looks great on the Fiesta saucer. Could it be this was another "Harmony" set that HLC didn't advertise in a national medium? Besides the primary-color trims we've mentioned, we've had a single report of some pieces with brown trim and some with no trim at all.

Plate 201B

Plate 201A
Very rare Mexicana plate using Liberty shape.

Plate 201B
Swing Demitasse Cups and Saucers; Teacup and Saucer.

Plate 202
Platter, 13½"; Sugar Bowl and Creamer; Baker, 9"; Lug Soup Bowl.

Plate 203
Kitchen Kraft Cake Plate; Covered Jug; Stacking Refrigerator Units and Lid; Salt and Pepper Shakers.

Plate 202

Plate 203

Plate 204
Teapot; Cup and Saucer; Deep 1-Pint Bowl.

Plate 205
Covered Casserole.

Plate 206
Batter Set.
    Decaled Century lines from the early '30s (such as English Garden or Columbine) often include batter sets, but here's one from a mid-to-late '30s line, Mexicana. Adding to the intrigue is the fact that the larger jug is dated "D-35" (April 1935), a full two years before HLC put this decal into general use! The smaller syrup jug is not dated but we assume from the creamier color of its glaze, that it's a later production. The two jugs were not found together, but nevertheless make a nice pair.

Photo © Adam Anik

Plate 204

Plate 205

Plate 206

Plate 207

Virginia Rose — this time as a very rare variation of the Mexicana line.
    Shown are the 9½" and 6" plates, teacup and saucer, and the 5" fruit bowl.

Plate 208

Nautilus "Eggshell."
    Pieces shown here are dated 1937. Note the blue-line trim and the stark white background. This line is very, very rare.
    Shown are the 13" platter, 9" and 7" plates, 5" fruit, creamer and sugar bowl, and the teacup and saucer.

Plate 207

Plate 208

Hacienda

This is a rather extensive line and is probably second only to Mexicana in availability. Both patterns are on Century shapes with few exceptions. Unlike Mexicana, however, you'll find no matching Kitchen Kraft line for Hacienda. However, at least one large Kitchen Kraft mixing bowl has been found, apparently a special order by a Birmingham, Alabama, furniture store.

Plate 209
Butter Dish, ½-Lb.; Teapot; Cream Soup Bowl.
    All of these items are relatively hard to find. Because of the consistency with which these butter dishes have been used in Century-based lines, we originally assumed their shape to be Century. The butter bottom even looks like Century because of its striped tab-like extensions; but if you'll look at the La Hacienda pattern on the Jade shape shown in Plate 359, you'll see that they're actually Jade instead. The Hacienda teapot turns up more often than its matching casserole. The reverse is true of Century Mexicana, and only the casserole has been reported in Century Conchita.

Plate 210
Plate, 10"; Fruit Bowl, 5"; Cup and Saucer; Creamer and Sugar Bowl.

Plate 209

Plate 210

125

Plate 211
Dinner Bell, Butter Dish.
　The bell has the Hacienda decal, but it's very doubtful that it was produced by HLC. The round butter dish is hard to find; this piece we guarantee to be Century.

Plate 212
Covered Jug.
　Because this piece is complete with the lid, it's twice as nice. This is a rare item.

Plate 213
Casserole.
　This is the regular Century casserole. It's a large, very attractive item, and extremely hard to find.

Plate 214
　This is a better view of the lovely and very elusive Nautilus casserole shown in the next photograph.

Plate 211

Plate 212

Plate 213

Plate 214

Plate 215
Nautilus Deep Plate; Platter, 13"; Plate 9"; Casserole; Creamer and Sugar Bowl; Sauce Boat; Teacup and Saucer.
　　Hacienda on the Nautilus shape is rare, and the line is doubly unusual in that the color is white, not ivory.

Plate 216
Swing Creamer and Sugar Bowl; Utility Tray; Casserole With Lid; Luncheon and Bread and Butter Plates; Fruit Bowl; Cup and Saucer; Platter, 11½"; Covered Sauce Bowl With Saucer; Salt and Pepper Shakers.
　　This is another rare example of the Hacienda decal applied to one of Homer Laughlin's standard dinnerware shapes other than Century; and again, the background color is white. Mexicana and Conchita also appear on Swing (not shown).

Plate 215

Plate 216

Photo © Adam Anik

127

Conchita

Conchita is a line that utilizes Century shapes. A fairly extensive line of Kitchen Kraft was offered as well, though collectors tell us that it's not as plentiful as Kitchen Kraft with the Mexicana decal. Virtually all Conchita is trimmed in red.

Plate 217

Platter, 11½"; Creamer and Sugar Bowl; Cup and Saucer.

These tumblers were featured in the Fiesta Ensembles (see Plate 273). They look especially good with the Mexican lines. There were two sets — one comprised of the three directly in front of the platter. A second set consisted of the one to the far left, a larger tumbler with the Fiesta dancing girl, and a small juice glass with a guitar. These fired-on designs can be found on both plain and lightly paneled glasses. A third set along with a matching pitcher is shown in the chapter called "Go-Alongs."

Plate 218

Kitchen Kraft Server; Underplate; Individual Casserole.

Notice the original label on the underplate. This is a decaled version of the elusive underplate that we've shown for the first time in this edition in the chapter on Fiesta Kitchen Kraft.

Plate 217

Plate 218

Plate 219
OvenServe Casserole; OvenServe Underplate; Cake Plate; Covered Jar; Covered Jug.
   The casserole is marked Handy Andy on the base; and although it's hard to see in the photo, there is an embossed design at the rim of the lid as well as around the outside of the underplate above it. These two pieces were found together, complete with the metal base — a rare find. You'll find this casserole with other decals, one a wheat and flower motif.

Plate 220
Kitchen Kraft Jars, Small, Medium, and Large; Salt and Pepper Shakers.
   The shakers are turned to show the decals on both sides.

Plate 219

Plate 220

Max-i-cana

We've never found an official name for this pattern anywhere in the company's files, but it's been dubbed "Max-i-cana" by collectors. The siesta-taking Mexican snoozing under his sombrero amid jugs, jars, and cacti decorate the shape known as "Yellowstone" in Plate 222 and looks just as much at home on ivory Fiesta in Plate 221.

Plate 221
Fiesta Max-i-cana Platter; Cup and Saucer; 4¾" Fruit.

Plate 222
Yellowstone Max-i-cana Platter; Sauce Boat Liner; Sauce Boat; Egg Cup; Rolled-Edge Egg Cup; Casserole; ½-lb. Butter Dish; Creamer and Sugar Bowl.
　　The platter measures 13½"; directly in front of it, the sauce bowl liner is 8½" long. A teapot has never been reported.

Plate 221

Plate 222

Plates 223 and 224

Yellow Harlequin Mexicali.

Until the seventh edition, Virginia Rose was the only shape we knew that was decorated with the Mexicali decal. These pictures show a set of yellow Harlequin Mexicali. This must have been a very exciting acquisition. Not a single other piece has ever surfaced that we know of, but the owner was lucky enough to buy the set intact.

Plate 225

11½" Platter; Creamer and Sugar Bowl.

Swing is the shape shown here with the 11½" platter decorated in the Mexicali pattern. The creamer and sugar bowl are in the Conchita design. All pieces are marked "Eggshell," a term used to indicate HLC's lightweight semiporcelain.

Plate 223

Plate 224

Plate 225

Plate 226
Virginia Rose.
　　Shown here with the Mexicali decal. You'll have to look long and hard for an example of this line or the two shown previously. All are extremely rare.

Plate 226

Ranchera

Plate 227
Nautilus Shape.
　　This final south-of-the-border dinnerware line utilizes the Nautilus shape again, this time with a decal we've never seen before. We have no knowledge of its official name, but the collector who is sharing this find with us suggests we call it "Ranchera."

Plate 227

Go-Alongs

"Go-alongs" is a term that has been coined by collectors to refer to metal parts (frames, handles, etc.) wooden-ware, flatware, linens, and a variety of other products whose style and colors were obviously made to accessorize the colored dinnerware lines that were made by HLC as well as many other companies. This aspect of collecting is very popular with many, but others feel that it has been given too much publicity. Their main concern is that because it's in "the book," it is often tagged "Fiesta" and sold as such when, of course, it is not. We must remember that Homer Laughlin was in the business to make dinnerware — not appliances, metal bowls, or any of the other items you will see in this section. The Fiesta patent was issued for the manufacture of nothing but dinnerware; so no matter what else you may encounter that carries the name "Fiesta," please don't be fooled into believing it to be the genuine article! For instance, you'll see a Fiesta Quikut flatware set in Plate 258. It would look great with your genuine Fiesta, but Fiesta it's not! And a reader has sent in a photo of her "Fiesta" tablecloth (Plate 260). Though the logo is very similar, the style of the lettering is entirely different, and the dancing girl is facing you. Beware! We have known of schemes meant to mislead collectors by using fake Fiesta ink stamps on items HLC never even dreamed of making!

Accessories shown in Plates 228 and 229 are decidedly Mexican in flavor, and their bright primary colors would be great with any of Homer Laughlin's solid-color dinnerware lines in the more vivid tones. The water set is decorated on one side with a dancing senorita and on the other with a guitar-strumming Mexican fellow. There are other lines of glassware that are compatible with either the '50s colors of Fiesta or Rhythm: water tumblers and juice tumblers with narrow bands of color in gray, dark green, chartreuse, and burgundy.

Plate 228
Water Set.
You'll find the tumblers in three sizes: 4¾" (8-oz.), 3¾" (8-oz.), and 3¾" (4-oz.) The pitcher holds 64 ounces and is 9½" tall.

Plate 229
Wooden Napkin Rings; Placecard Holders; Cord-wrapped Enameled Tumblers; Coasters in a Wireware Frame.
These items could certainly create a party atmosphere when mixed, for instance, with a setting of Riviera.

Plate 228

Plate 229

While we once thought the metal fittings for the cream soup bowl, the marmalade, and the cake plate (in Plate 232) were most certainly marketed by an outside company, we now have a photocopy of a company order sheet that shows not only these but the "#610 salad service set" pictured in Plate 233. The photocopy also shows the three items in the line drawings below: the condiment set — mustard, salt and pepper shakers; the "#608 8" casserole" (the promotional casserole, see Plate 9); and "#609 double tidbit with folding stand." Since we first pictured these drawings, several of the casserole frames have turned up (some with minor variations), but as far as we know, the stand on the right has yet to be found. These items comprise their "#600 Gift Assortment of Colored Ware"; and because the colors listed are red, green, blue, and yellow, we assume that these were offered in the early days of production. There is another frame that will hold both the marmalade and the mustard; it's not shown in this edition. And you may find a metal rotating base that turns the six-part Fiesta relish tray into a Lazy-Susan server.

Plate 230

Dessert Service for Eight.

 A few years ago a collector sent us this photo. The service contains 7" Fiesta plates, two each in red, cobalt, yellow, and green, accompanied by glass tumblers and sherbets to match. The glassware is of good quality, and while the cobalt, yellow, and green are transparent, the red appears to have been fired on. She was able to trace it back to the '40s when an HLC employee gave it to a friend as a wedding gift.

Plate 230

Plate 231
Rattan Holders.
    Dyed to match Fiesta tumblers.

Plate 232
Cream Soup Bowl; Marmalade;
    Chop Plate with Metal Fittings.

Plate 233
#610 Salad Service Set.

Plate 231

Plate 232

Plate 233

Plate 234

Three-tier Tidbit Tray.

This piece bears need for a little discussion. Obviously if the metal fittings were available, either old or newly made, anyone could create this item. This one has the ring handle which some collectors feel is the "correct" handle, but you'll also find some with the triangular terminal such as you can see on the Amberstone tray in our color plates — it's also shown in the company's Amberstone advertising material in our files. We questioned a long-time dealer who agrees that when buying this piece, you should inspect it carefully; these were being made with new fittings by an individual only a few years ago.

Plates 235 – 238

Decaled Tumbler; Nut Dish; another Nut Dish; Two-tier Tidbit.

Harlequin and Riviera have had their fair share of metal enhancements as well. Plates 235 through 238 attest to that. The decaled tumbler is fitted with a chrome soda-fountain-style base and handle, and we call the Harlequin 36s bowl a nut dish — it was made by some enterprising company simply by adding a little chrome and a glass knob! Note the hardware on the ivory Century/Riviera items. It's identical to the Harlequin nut dish down to the glass ball finials. All three items are obviously the work of the same company. The two-tier tidbit is usually found only in ivory, but one has also been found in green, complete with a green glass knob. Whether or not at some time these were marketed by HLC is anybody's guess at this point, but personally, we doubt it. But there were evidently promotions offered by the company for which there are no documentation, so who is to say!

Plate 235

Plate 236

Plate 234

Plate 237

Plate 238

In the early 1940s, the Hankscraft Company marketed their electric egg cooker in service sets that included the cooker as shown in Plate 239, "four vari-colored Fiesta egg cups (red, yellow, blue, and green), ivory (pottery) poaching dish, Fiesta salt and pepper shakers, and maple plywood tray." They called this set the "Fiesta Egg Service" and sold it for $9.50 to $13.70, depending upon whose catalog you happened to be using. The set as shown has not been listed in any of these catalogs but is the one more often found. Obviously, these egg cups are not Fiesta. They're made of the same vitrified material as the cooker itself (which is identical to the one pictured with the Fiesta set mentioned above) and are smaller than genuine Fiesta egg cups. The colors are fired on, and in addition to the red example shown here, the cooker has also been found in green and yellow. Remember, this was a Hankscraft product — not made by Homer Laughlin, not genuine Fiesta!

A similar idea found in a gift-giving ad from a Christmas 1937 *American Home* magazine featured a Westinghouse sandwich grill on a tray large enough to accommodate it, a small cutting board, and several pieces of Fiesta: the utility tray with what appears in the photograph to be the center relish tray insert nestled in one end, a stack of small plates, salt and pepper shakers, a mustard, and a marmalade.

Plate 239
Electric Egg Cooker; Egg Cups; Poaching Dish.

Plate 240
"Fiesta" Popcorn Set.
   This is enameled tinware marketed during the '40s (as far as we know, not by HLC). Note the familiar Fiesta-type rings and colors. Recently we heard from a collector in Arizona who found the whole popcorn set still in its original carton marked Snack Set #90 US Mfg Crop, Decatur, IL, wrapped in the old packing paper. She found not only these bowls, but also a matching 20"x60" yellow-enameled metal tray, an ivory Fiesta creamer, probably for the melted butter, and a yellow Fiesta salt shaker. The auctioneer said that there had been a wooden spoon that had disappeared from the box.

Plate 239

Plate 240

Plates 241 and 242

Beverage Carriers and Other Accessories.

The carrier in Plate 241 is wrought iron; the one in Plate 242 is wireware. As far as we know, these were not marketed by HLC; but since we now know the company actually sold more of these accessories than we once thought they did, we hesitate to seem entirely confident about it either way. Watch for reproductions of the carrier in Plate 241. Also in Plate 242, the teapot is converted to a dripolator with the addition of the 5½" metal assembly. Reticulated metal holders with handles like the one above the teapot are shown on a second photocopy we have advertising the "#109-12 Assortment Package." It includes the 10" KK pie plate and platter, the 8½" and 9½" Fiesta nappies, and the promotional casserole. These photocopies along with the fact that the promotional casserole (shown in Plate 9) was found in an unopened carton convinced us that this casserole was really an HLC product, even though the company told us years ago that it was not. The large Fiestawood piece was made by the G.H. Specialty Co., Milwaukee, Wisconsin.

Plate 243

Center Insert for Lazy-Susan

This is the center insert for the 20" Fiestawood piece shown in Plate 242. It's from a line called Intaglio, made by Indiana Glass during the 1930s. It measures 10" in diameter.

Plate 241

Plate 242

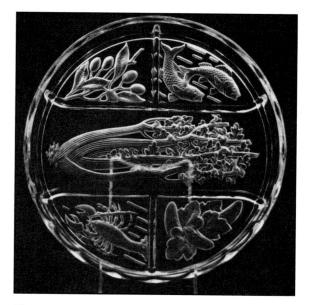

Plate 243

Plate 244
Code Numbers.
See Kitchen Cabinet in Plate 246.

Plate 245
Tidbit.
This item features the same type of metal bowls as the "Fiesta" Popcorn Set in a cloverleaf wireware stand.

Plate 246
Kitchen Cabinet; Tinware Canisters; Breadbox; Cake Cover.
We've hear of some strange things, but none has ever topped the kitchen cabinet shown here. Note the red, green, cobalt, and yellow trim. The Hoosier-type cabinet has a porcelain work surface, flour sifter, and utensil and bread drawers. Attached side cabinets house storage shelves. Each piece is marked with code numbers and "Fiesta." Detective work by the current owner located the manufacturer, the Marsh Furniture Company of High Point, North Carolina, who is still in business today. Their sales manager said it was common at the time for Marsh to special order a variation of their cabinets for large customers such as Montgomery Ward or J.C. Penney. With the introduction of Fiesta by HLC in 1936, he assumed the special order may have been a marketing tie-in by one of their retailers or even possibly for a store display. All tinware accessory items pictured are stamped Tindeco, once a major tin products company in Baltimore.

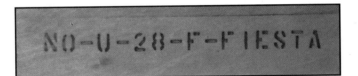

Plate 244

Plate 245

Plate 246

Plates 247 and 248
Fiestawood.
   Wooden go-alongs are popular with collectors. These two are salad bowls — note the brightly colored band of rings that is characteristic of all Fiestawood we have seen.

Plate 249
Fiestawood.
   Woodenware by an unidentified company; paired with the revolving metal base and a 15" Fiesta chop plate, it becomes a Lazy-Susan. We've also seen nappies in fruit-decorated wooden holders.

Plate 250
Fiestawood Party Server.
   The mushroom-shaped center section is for hors d'oeuvres; it's pierced to hold toothpicks, and it can be removed.

Plate 247

Plate 249

Plate 248

Plate 250

Plate 251

Ice Bucket.
 Rattan-wrapped handles have been found to accessorize several items. This example has been fitted to a mixing bowl, creating an ice bucket. It's an exact match to the metal handle offered in combination with the chop plate in the 1939–43 selling campaign. These have been found in sizes to fit the 7", 9", and 10" plates (which also fits the relish tray) as well as both sizes of the chop plates. We'd almost bet these were routed through HLC!

Plate 252

Hors d'oeuvres Tray.
 The fish in the center is pierced to hold toothpicks. The border decoration is especially effective — stripes in festive colors punctuated by decals of a snoozing Mexican.

Plate 253

Do-it-yourself Decals.
 These were readily available in 5-and-10¢ stores, and collectors have reported finding sheets of them such as the one shown here. The back of the sheet reads "Designs by Betty Best, Festivalware, Set #5001." They were produced in 1945 by the American Decalcomania Co. of Chicago and New York. You may find tiles that have been commercially decorated with these decals, and shelf paper by Betty Brite that also features Fiesta dishes.

Plate 251

Plate 253

Plate 252

Plates 254 – 257

Tin Kitchenware.

Items such as these were popular during the late '30s and '40s. One company who made them was Owens-Illinois Can Co. They called their line "Fiesta" (what else) and decorated it in "Roman stripes in red, blue, and green on yellow." The set consisted of canisters, a bread box, a dust pan, a garbage can, a wastebasket (14½" tall) and a kitchen stool. As you can see, some of these tinware items were decaled with Fiesta-like dinnerware. A three-tiered vegetable bin has been found to match. The breadbox in Plate 256 is decorated in pots and plants with a Mexican flavor. In our files we have a photo of a 12" turquoise chop plate to which has been added a tinware cake-safe top. The lid is enameled in a matching turquoise, and it's topped with a wooden knob.

Plate 254   Photo by Ann Wise

Plate 255

Plate 256

Plate 257

Plate 258

Catalin-Handled Stainless Steel Flatware.

The "Fiesta Ensemble" (see Plate 273) offered by the company in the early years of production included a set of flatware with Catalin (plastic) handles, color coordinated to match the dinnerware. Several other patterns of Catalin-handled cutlery were on the market during this period — an especially intriguing set is shown here (note the name on the box). Collectors love to use this type of flatware to recreate the "Ensemble" look. Prices vary greatly — if you buy it a piece at a time, you should be able to buy at much lower prices proportionately than if you purchase a place setting, especially if salad forks or tablespoons are included. Boxed sets that contain service for eight or more with several extra serving pieces go at a premium.

Plate 259

Tea Set.

This set will be as close as you'll get to a "Fiesta" children's tea set, but this one never saw the light of day at HLC. It's marked "Made in Japan." We show the teapot, creamer and sugar bowl, but also included in the service for six were plates, cups, and saucers.

Plate 258

Plate 259

Plate 260

Tablecloth.

    Vintage linens that color coordinate with the primary hues favored by HLC abound, and collectors love them all. Some have matching napkins. Depending on size and condition, these generally fall into the $25.00 to $45.00 price range. The tablecloth shown here may carry the Fiesta name, but it's bogus! HLC didn't make or distribute table linens.

Plate 261

Ash Stand.

    Just about as unlikely as a kitchen cabinet is this ash stand. The design of the metal stand is right out of the '50s, and so is the Fiesta deep plate in chartreuse.

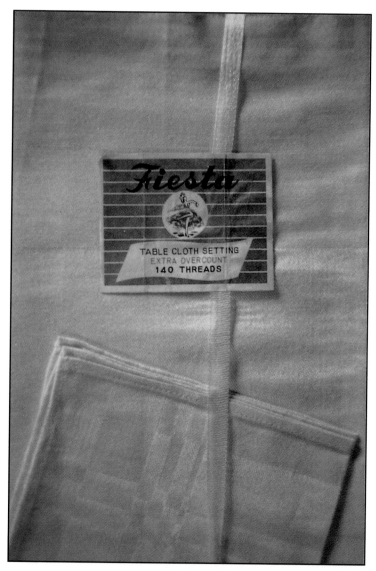

Plate 260

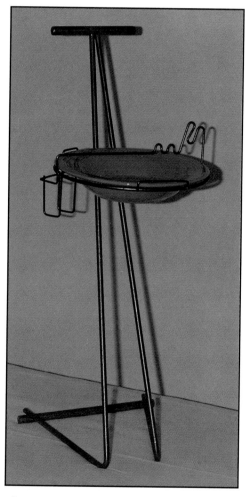

Plate 261

~~ *Commercial Adaptations and Ephemera* ~~

Advertising materials — especially HLC's own — make interesting and desirable additions to our collections, and they're certainly worthwhile investments as well! The company's price lists contain a wealth of information. They've been our main source of study, and as new ones are found to fill in the gaps, we may yet learn more. Because most of them are dated, we have been able to learn when items were introduced or dropped, what colors were in production during a given year, and occasionally we would pick up a tidbit of information that would help in answering one of our many questions. Fiesta price lists, though by no means easy to find, come up for sale much more often those that represent the company's other lines.

Two of these lists are shown in Plate 262, and in the following several plates you'll see Riviera, Fiesta Kitchen Kraft, and Harlequin price lists. There's also a very rare Jubilee price list shown earlier in this book (see page 105).

Plate 262
Fiesta Price List.

Plate 262

Plate 263
Epicure Price List (Front).

Plate 263

Plate 264
Epicure Price List (Back).

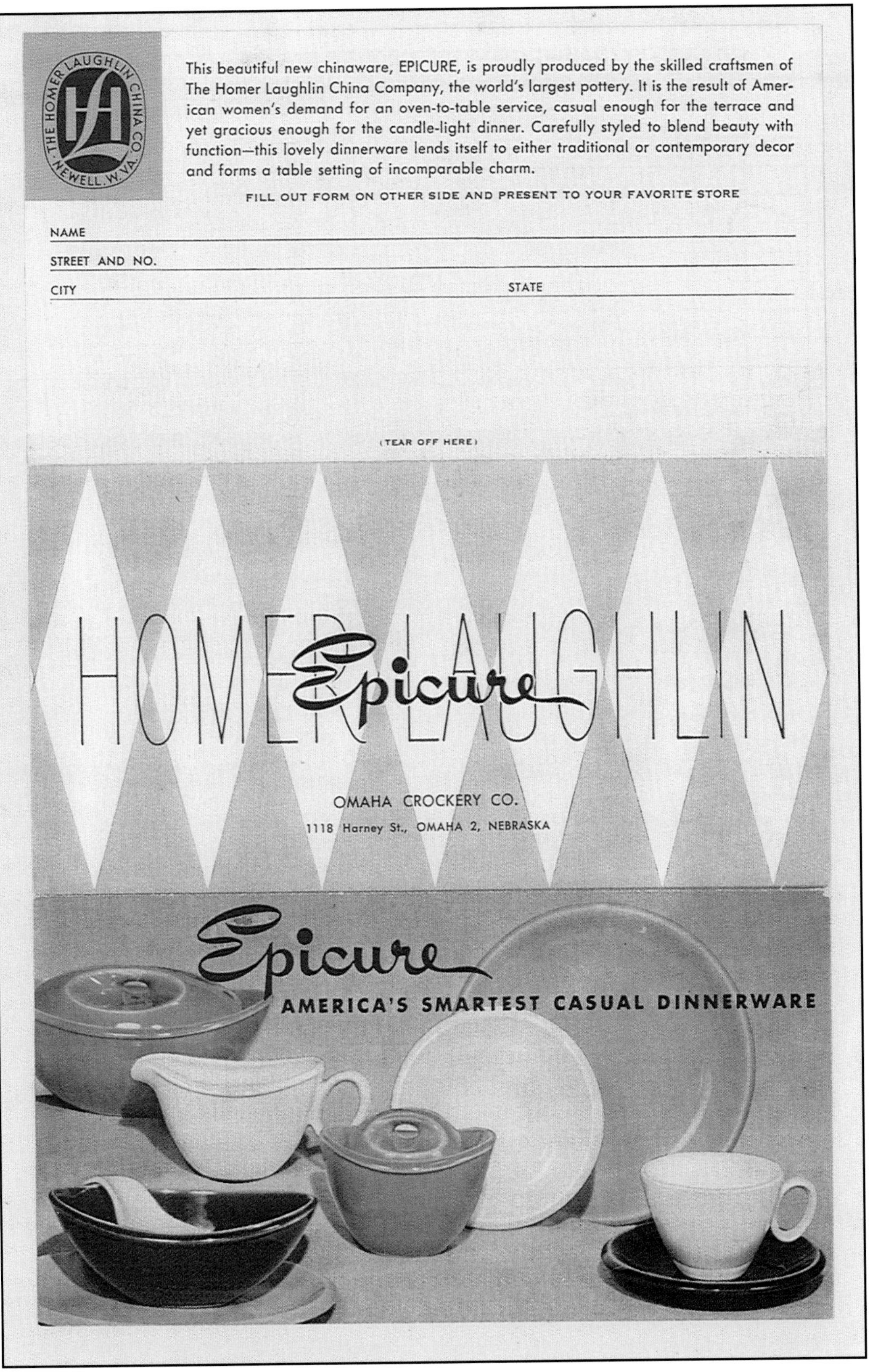

Plate 264

Plate 265
Riviera Price List.

Plate 266
Fiesta Kitchen Kraft Price List.

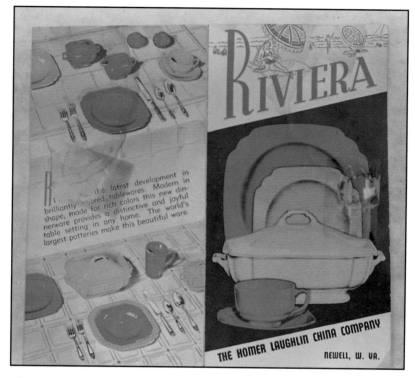

Plate 265

Plate 266

Plate 267
Harlequin Price List.

Plate 268
Fiesta Kitchen Kraft Store Display.

This cardboard store display captures and conveys the festive appeal of Fiesta dinnerware. This particular one never left the HLC pottery, but a few collectors report being lucky enough to have found one elsewhere. There were actually two of the small side sections; one is missing from this example. You can judge its size from the mixing bowls on either side. A collector sent us a photo of another display, this one of Spanish ladies dancing down a cobblestone piazza with a big villa in the background and a guitar player to the left — all recessed behind a large archway and a platform for the Fiesta.

Plate 267

Plate 268

149

Plates 269 – 271
Original Packaging Material.
   Examples such as these are very popular with collectors — especially those with the dancing girl logo. Imagine finding the four-place dinner service still mint in the box. The sugar bowl and creamer in Plate 270 are special enough on their own, they're medium green! But factor in the original packaging, and they're fantastic.

Plate 269

Plate 270

Plate 271

Plate 272

Ad for the "Juanita Dinner Ensemble."

For several years, we've described the Juanita beverage set in the Riviera section, but this is the first time we've had the opportunity to show this ad. This particular ad appeared as a full-page display in the *Indianapolis Star* dated November 6, 1938. It offers "119 Piece Juanita Dinner Ensemble by the Makers of Fiestaware." Though it includes forty-eight pieces of Riviera, the line name isn't mentioned anywhere in the ad. A similar ad appears in Plate 273.

Plate 273

"Fiesta Ensemble."

Described in an earlier chapter, this ensemble was offered in only four basic colors along with matching Mexican glassware tumblers. A collector who owns a copy of this ad describes the ashtray/coasters shown above the table as "clear glass — no design, except a waffle pattern." Note the interesting blend of Fiesta and Riviera. These ensembles were boxed and shipped from the factory with the glassware and flatware, and very often furniture companies gave them as a bonus to their customers when they made a major purchase, such as a bedroom or living room set. Some collectors feel that this Fiesta Ensemble may have been the source for at least some of the cobalt Riviera plates. There was at least one other Ensemble — this one contained only Fiesta dinnerware, a service for six plus the same basic serving pieces shown here, as well as identical glassware and flatware. It was offered as a prize in an essay contest sponsored by a paint store.

Plate 272

Plate 273

If you enjoy collecting advertising ephemera, try to find the October 10, 1936, issue of *The Saturday Evening Post*. Inside is a beautiful two-page Armstrong floor covering ad with a vintage kitchen-dining room fairly blooming with Fiesta. Another ad featuring Fiesta appeared in *Better Homes and Gardens*, December 1936. *Household Magazine*, September 1937, has a full page of quick and easy luncheon recipes. The picture shows an uncovered Fiesta casserole full of onion soup, and three uncovered onion soup bowls sitting around it.

Several years ago, the Dard Mfg. Co. of Evanston, Illinois, produced an item that for awhile caused a bit of excitement in the Fiesta world. In a box marked "Fiesta Coasters, Tag-Master Line ASI 4850" — exactly the right size to hold the relish tray center — they marketed a set of four plastic advertising coasters. Someone less than honest tried to perpetuate the "Fiesta Coaster Hoax" by replacing the plastic coasters with the relish center. So be on guard, though this sort of thing doesn't happen much anymore, since today's collectors are much better informed than we were when Fiesta collecting was in its infancy.

The ashtray seems to have been a popular item for advertising use. In previous issues we've shown others. One of our favorites was the gold-lettered cobalt example we saw in the early 1970s in the conference room at HLC, and though we looked for years for one to buy, we never found it.

Plate 274
Ashtray.
   This carries not only the Fiesta ink stamp on the back but the name of the Sears, Roebuck Company as well.

Plate 275
Fiesta Kitchen Kraft Pie Plate.
   This is an ivory 9" pie plate that was a grocery store giveaway more than fifty years ago. The plate behind it is in a non-standard color — Harlequin spruce green.

Plates 276 – 279
Fiesta Fruit Bowl, Plate, Egg Cup, and Tumbler.
   For several years the Lazarus Company issued Fiesta items to commemorate their anniversaries. Here are four of them, a fruit bowl for their 87th year, a plate for their 88th, an egg cup for their 89th, and a tumbler for their 90th.

Plate 280
Syrup Base.
   This is still full of the Dutchess brand tea that was sold in it many years ago; the label and the cork stopper are completely intact — what a rare and interesting find!

Plate 274

Plate 275

Plate 276

Plate 277

Plate 278

Plate 279

Plate 280

The commercial uses of Fiesta in advertising and television have become so commonplace that we can't even think of them all — alongside featured recipes and cereal ads in leading women's magazines, in the kitchens of many TV sitcom homes, on product containers, on the covers of cookbooks, and so forth. And if it's Taco Bell trying to tempt you with some mouth-watering south-of-the-border food, it's a given it'll be displayed on a Fiesta plate or platter. But how about "Fiesta Wear, ladies' blouses dyed to match those dishes." I'm not making this up! We saw this ad several years ago, but only once, so it evidently didn't catch right on! Plates 281 through 284 are examples of only a few commercial applications. Though most of the time it's Fiesta that's featured, other colored dinnerware lines have been used as well. A few years ago we received a greeting card with three luscious fuchsia tulips whose long stems curve forward from the lip of a yellow disk pitcher — even Hallmark can appreciate the wonderful Art Deco lines of Fiesta; it's as striking today as it was when Rhead designed it, more than sixty years ago. What a tribute to his talent.

Plate 281
Soup Can Label.
   Harlequin is featured; shown here is a medium green cream soup bowl.

Plate 282
Punch-outs.
   These were distributed by the National Dairy Council during the 1950s. Originally there were eight in the series, but they were reissued in the '60s, and four more were added for a total of twelve.

Plate 283
Recipe File.

Plate 284
Seed Packet.
   Riviera is featured.

Plate 281

Plate 283

Plate 282

Plate 284

Collectors have reported a variety of advertising mugs — one decorated with a caricature of Lucille Ball signed "Love, Lucy"; from the Desilu Studios sounds especially unique. The Jackson Custom China Co. of Falls Creek, Pennsylvania, once made mugs similar to the Tom and Jerry. We've heard of them in brown with a cream interior and (hold on to your hats) maroon! How'd you like a set of those for your morning coffee! These were evidently not made on any large scale, but in case you should see some of them around, don't be taken in. The same company also produced a child's set consisting of a divided plate, a 6" bowl, and the Tom and Jerry, all in white decorated with a blue stenciled Donald Duck and friends.

T and Js in Fiesta colors with advertising are rare, though it isn't uncommon to find examples with color on the inside only (and some will be found without the advertising). These were produced during the late '60s into the early '70s; interior colors are turquoise, yellow, rose, amberstone, or turf green.

Plate 285
Advertising Mugs
   White, not ivory, is the color of these mugs.

Plate 286
Coasters.
   These accompanied the mugs shown in Plate 287 and are very hard to find.

Plate 285

Plate 286

156

Plate 287

Series of Six Mugs.

These were distributed at annual meetings of Buick Management and their Retirement Club members, 1964 through 1969. Represented on the mugs are a 1924 Model 48 Buick, a 1904 Model B Buick, a 1936 Buick Special, a 1941 Buick Roadmaster, a 1908 Model 10 Buick, and a 1916 Model D Buick. Plate 286 illustrates the coasters that accompanied them; these are hard to find.

Plate 288

Ashtray.

Inscription reads, "1963 Buick Management Meeting, Dec. 11-12." It is 8¾" in diameter and has six cigarette rests.

Plate 289

Advertising Mug.

This is the new-style mug; it was presented by the State of West Virginia to commemorate the introduction of the newly redesigned Fiesta Ware line.

Plate 287

Plate 288

Plate 289

157

A Word to the Wise

As any collector of colored dinnerware knows, there are many lines with characteristics very similar to Homer Laughlin's. Not just Fiesta, but in fact nearly any of HLC's solid-color patterns has a look-alike. Potteries made a practice of reproducing each other's colors and designs, especially those that had proven to be successful on the market. For instance, Bauer's Monterey (1934) is very similar to Fiesta in both color and design. The cake stand shown in Plate 293 is a good example of that line. The band of rings, weight, and feel of this piece might cause even a seasoned collector to have second thoughts. In addition to the turquoise shown, Monterey also came in maroon, yellow, green, orange-red, medium blue, and ivory. Bauer's earlier line called Ring (1932), though with chunkier, heavier lines, was also produced in the bright solid glazes.

Serenade's counterpart was Lu-Ray by Taylor, Smith & Taylor. Pastel colors and simple lines were characteristic of both. Rhythm had a twin in Universal's Ballerina line. W.S. George made Rainbow, which is very easily confused with HLC's Tango line. And many other companies, among them Vernon Kilns, Franciscan, Metlox, Coors, and French Saxon China, produced solid-color dinnerware as well.

Plate 290

Teapots.

This photo contains a wonderful array of shapes and colors. These teapots represent lines that were Fiesta's contemporaries; they were produced by various manufacturers, all located in Ohio. The green pot is Taylor, Smith & Taylor's Vistosa, a line styled with pastry-crimped rims and handles daintily trimmed with tiny blossoms. Vistosa was made in Fiesta-like red, cobalt blue, yellow, and light green. Caliente (the cobalt teapot) was made by Paden City; its streamlined styling featured hollow ware whose bases were designed with four petal-like feet, and its colors were identical to Vistosa's. The large red teapot (top right) is Valencia by Shawnee, and the smaller red pot (bottom right) is part of Knowles' Yorktown line.

Plate 290

Photo © Adam Anik

158

Even the Mexican decaled lines had competition. Stetson made Mexicalis, Paden City had Patio, Mt. Clemons produced Old Mexico, and Tia Juana was a line by the Knowles Company. So it is obvious that it takes a certain amount of study and caution to become a knowledgeable collector. To become familiar with the lines mentioned above, we recommend *The Collector's Encyclopedia of American Dinnerware* by Jo Cunningham. If you are a beginning collector intending to limit your buying to a particular line of Homer Laughlin's, use this book as your guideline. It would be rare (though not entirely impossible) to find an authentic, previously undiscovered item that by now we have not shown, thanks to the faithfulness of our readers in reporting such finds, so be extremely suspicious.

Even today, dinnerware companies continue to produce lines that draw on Fiesta's Art Deco appeal. In Plate 291 is a line by Mikasa called Moderna, designed by Larry Laslo. This line was carried by some of the larger mail-order firms in 1985 and '86. It was available in several colors; each piece is marked Mikasa. White "Fiesta" has been featured in restaurants located in Rockefeller Center by Restaurant Associates who commissioned Rego China of Whitestone, Queens, to make the ware for them. Nineteen pieces were designed; although none of the original molds were used, the style is unmistakable.

Our advice? Be cautious! If you're a beginning collector and haven't seen or handled Fiesta firsthand, find a dealer. Study his merchandise, and study this book. We welcome your inquiries if you have questions concerning identification. If there are new discoveries — and there may yet be — we will do our best to keep you informed and up to date!

Plate 291
Fiesta-Inspired, Moderna Dinnerware by Mikasa.
Note the ring handles on the cups and the sugar bowl.

Plate 292
Fiesta-like Cup.
The collector who reported this Fiesta fraud chose this cup from among several that were probably genuine, because it seemed to be in better shape than some of the others. When he got home with it, he noticed that it was slightly smaller and lighter and that there were abnormalities in the shape of the bowl and the handle. On closer examination he found that it was faintly marked "England."

Plate 292

Plate 291

Plate 293

Other HLC Look-alikes.

The bud vase, with an obviously inferior glaze, is just enough smaller to indicate that it has been cast from a mold made from an original. The little disk pitcher really is not from a child's set of Fiesta, even though its color and design suggest that it might well be. The cobalt pitcher looks very much like the Harlequin novelty creamer, but it has no band of rings. The donkey may look like its Harlequin double but sometimes pulls a cart marked "California." In the background in the Bauer cake stand mentioned earlier.

Plate 294

Pitcher.

Marked Fiesta (see Plate 295), it was marketed by Franciscan in the late 1970s, part of a line called "Kaleidoscope." But according to Deleen Enge in the book *Franciscan: Plain and Fancy*, the serving pieces that went with the line were called "Fiesta." These pitchers have been reported to us in white, yellow, cobalt, and gray-blue, but according to Enge, the color assortment included cocoa, tangerine, dark green, and a color they called Sandman as well.

Plate 295

Pitcher (Bottom).

Notice the Fiesta mark.

Plate 293

Plate 294

Plate 295

Plate 296

Refrigerator Jar.

This looks very much like the KK stacking unit in color as well as weight, though it is much smaller in size. We haven't a clue as to its manufacturer. There are bulb-type candle holders very similar to Fiesta's, and salt and pepper shakers of many types. One curious set we once saw consisted of what appeared to be a genuine Fiesta salt shaker perched atop a little raised platform with handles which was actually the pepper! HLC had never heard of it!

Plate 297

Pie Plate.

This looks to be Harlequin, and collectors have long believed that it was an HLC product. It's been found in cobalt and light green, and the colors match HLC's exactly. We took one to the pottery years ago, and our Homer Laughlin contact assured us that they never made them; but now we have been told that a picture of this item has been found in the old company files. We'll have more on the subject next time.

Plate 296

Plate 297

The Morgue

Many years ago on one of our visits to HLC, we were allowed a rare treat — a visit to the dark secretive room hidden behind a locked and barred door in the uppermost niche of the office building that somehow down through the years earned the name "the morgue." Dark and dingy it might have been, but to a collector of HLC dinnerware, it was filled with excitement! We were allowed to dig through boxes and shelves where we found fantastic experimentals, beautiful trial glazes, and unfamiliar modifications of standard forms. On our second visit some years later, we returned with a professional photographer through whose photos we are able to share the fun with all of you. All the photos in this chapter are from the morgue. All of these wonderful pieces are company property, and many of them are now on display at the factory outlet museum in Newell.

One item we especially liked on our first trip through the morgue was a vase that was out on loan when we made our return visit. We've yet to have the opportunity to photograph it ourselves, but we'll try to describe it for you. It was glazed in ivory with a 6" upright disk body that looked like the joined front halves of two juice pitchers without their ice guards. There was a stack of Fiesta plates in unbelievable trial glazes — a pink beige, a spatter effect in dark brown on orange, a smoky delphinium blue, a dark red grape that might possibly be the rose ebony referred to in Rhead's article, a dark russet, a deep mustard yellow, and our favorite — black with four chromium bands.

Plate 298
(Left to Right) Divided Relish, Carafe, Vase, Syrup, Ashtray, Divided Relish, Coffee Mug.
The divided relish is molded in one piece; it measures 11" in diameter and has the look of Fiesta. The carafe, 10" tall and glazed in Fiesta green, was actually produced for a buffet-ware line they called Kenilworth which was marketed by Marshall Fields during the mid-'50s. These have been found in Turquoise, Snow White, and Dawn Pink as well, and they carry the Kenilworth mark. A gold-tone metal neck sleeve with an angular handle and a cork-lined plastic stopper supplemented the pottery bottle. The Kenilworth line also utilized Rhythm and Cavalier shapes. In the center of the photo is a magnificent red Fiesta 12" vase over which wars would certainly be waged if it were up for grabs, which, of course, it is not. The piece to the right of the vase looks very familiar except for its size. It's 6½" tall, and its proportions exactly match the Fiesta syrup's. Directly in front of it is the only marked piece we saw in the morgue. Most experimentals were merely marked with a number or not at all. This one, however, was embossed "Fiesta" in the mold. It's 5" across and has the band of rings on the flange. The green relish section on the right was designed so that four would fit a large oval wooden tray. The coffee mug in yellow is 3" high and except for the short tapered base is exactly like the standard mug.

Plate 298

162

Other goodies that were out on loan during our second visit were two different styles of Harlequin candle holders that we had cataloged before. One pair was large and flat, 5½" in diameter with a 2½" tall candle cup in the center. The others were shaped like the large half of an inverted cone, 4¼" across the bottom, and 3" tall. Both styles were lovely but not quite as nice as our regular Harlequin candle holders. One of the most exciting Harlequin pieces we saw was a demitasse cup and saucer in a beautiful high-gloss black. Trial glaze plates included light chocolate, deep gray, delphinium blue, vanilla, caramel, black, and a luscious lavender.

We hope you have found this peek inside the morgue to be as much fun as it was for us to bring it to you. If you have the opportunity to visit Newell, be sure to stop at the company's museum. Many of these treasures are now on display there.

Plate 299

Fiesta Experimental: Individual Teapot.

This is one of the most beautiful and exciting pieces among the Fiesta experimentals. It's 6" high, and the lid is interchangeable with the standard demitasse pot. It was one of several pieces modeled by Fredrick Rhead, the designer, that was never marketed due to the onset of the war — in fact, many already existing lines had to be cut back. Though this teapot was never mass produced, at least three (all in ivory) have been accounted for.

Plate 300

Adaptations of the French Casserole and Bowl.

The French casserole is a footed version of the more familiar yellow one. The bowl measures 9¾" tall by 6" in diameter; the high foot that has been added nicely transforms a utilitarian mixing bowl into an elegant serving piece.

Plate 299

Plate 300

Plate 301

Harlequin Experimentals: Nappy, Sauce Cup, Deep Dish, Bowl.

The nappy is 4" across and is shaped like the small Fiesta fruits. Next, a sauce cup, perhaps, made from the demitasse cup mold. The deep dish in mauve blue is 2½" by 7" — it has the Harlequin rings inside. On the far right, the yellow bowl measures 2½" by 5½" in diameter.

Plate 302

(Left to Right) Plate, Sauce Dish, Footed Console Bowl, ¼-lb. Butter Dish, Plate.

The tall 6" Riviera candle holders we had fallen in love with on our first visit were on loan, but the footed console bowl was there for our photography session. It's huge — 3½" x 8½" x 13½" long! The ivory Century piece is a one-piece fast-stand sauce dish, 7" across the attached tray. A few of these have been found around the country since we first described this one to our readers, but they'd still be considered very scarce. Although the butter dish on the right is just the size to hold a quarter-pound stick of today's butter, this style was passed up in favor of the shorter quarter-pound version and the one-half pound size. This one was never marketed; it's 7½" long.

Plate 301

Plate 302

~ *Experimentals and Employees' Inventions* ~

In addition to the experimentals from the morgue, a few more very rare or one-of-a kind items have been found outside the factory. Those that were made from a specifically designed mold or glazed in a trial color we'll call experimentals; those that were glazed in non-regulation glazes or items that were put together at the whim of an imaginative employee, we'll call employees' inventions.

Plate 303
Jugs.
Shown is our regular two-pint jug alongside another that holds just one pint. This is the only one we've heard of and really have no information whatsoever on it.

Plate 304
Sugar Bowl.
This color is near-Wells Art Glaze brown. It is the same sugar bowl as the ivory example in Plate 306.

Plate 305
Harlequin Tumbler.
This has been fitted with a Riviera handle — a one-of-a-kind employee's invention.

Plate 306
Creamer and Sugar Bowl.
These unique items sit on the standard figure-8 tray. This set and another creamer have been found in ivory, and the same sugar bowl is shown in Plate 304 in a near-Wells Art Glaze brown.

Plate 303

Plate 304   Photo © Adam Anik

Plate 305

Plate 306

Plate 307
Chamberstick.
   The imagination of the employee who created this unique chamberstick was really on overtime! It's made from the stem of a sweets compote, a demitasse saucer, and, of course, you recognize the familiar Fiesta ring handle.

Plate 308
Sherbets.
   Unproduced though clearly marked in the mold, this pair of sherbets was made in swirling pastels. Was someone trying to imitate Niloak's Mission, using the blue Skytone clay, terra cotta from the Suntone line, and their standard white?

Plate 309
Set of Trial Glaze Harlequin 9" Plates.
   The owners describe the blue as being very similar to Skytone and the beige a good match for Jubilee.

Plate 307

Plate 308

Plate 309

Plate 310

10" Comport.

This is a scaled-down model of our standard 12" fruit comport. There are at least three collectors who have been lucky enough to find one of these.

Plate 311

Tom and Jerry Mug.

One mug from a maroon punch set containing twelve mugs and a large salad bowl all glazed to match. The set has been broken up now, and when a piece of it happens to hit the market, as it does now and then, it will be snapped up at a premium price.

Plate 312

Onion Soup.

Alongside the standard onion soup is (as far as we know) a one-of-a-kind variation that surfaced within the last ten years. Shown here in light green, it differs from the regular version in several ways: note that the handles are flat rather than rolled under, the bowl flares at the rim above the handles, and the foot is wider and shorter. The lid is less rounded and ½" wider. It's marked "Fiesta HLC" in the mold.

Plate 310

Plate 311

Plate 312

Plate 313

Sugar Bowls.

There are three distinct differences in these sugar bowls. The experimental is on the left, the standard sugar bowl on the right. In the experimental: 1) the base is raised and the inside bottom flat; 2) the width of the lip flange is twice as wide as the standard version; and 3) the mark is Fiesta, HLC, USA. This is the same mark that you'll find on the stick-handled creamer; another similarity to that piece is the flat inside bottom. The owner of this rare item says he believes this to be a very early design, possibly modeled as a companion to the stick-handled creamer, later modified to eliminate possible production problems.

Plate 314

Bowl.

The owners like to call this a "spaghetti bowl." It's shown in a relish base for size comparison. Under the flange on the outside is the familiar band of rings. It's 1⅜" deep and 10⅞" in diameter. It's unmarked, but almost certainly Fiesta.

Plate 315

6" Tray.

There's no doubt at all about this red tray. It was purchased several years ago in the Newell, West Virginia, area. The seller had used it under the syrup pitcher, saying that it fit perfectly. As you can see just by the photos in this chapter, most of these one-of-a-kind (or at least extremely limited) items have been found in ivory, and most are unmarked. So this piece is very unusual, not only in its rarity but also because of its red glaze, and to top it all off, it is marked Fiesta in the mold.

Plate 313

Plate 314

Plate 315

Plate 316

Lid.

This red lid fits the Kitchen Kraft stacking units perfectly, and that's about all we know about it. It may even have been designed for some other purpose — a hot plate, for instance, for the regular Fiesta line (the band of rings does seem out of step in Kitchen Kraft). This is the only one that's ever been reported.

Plate 317

9" Plate.

This mint green was a trial glaze — it bears a handwritten, underglaze identification code of "5971." Its owner describes it as "somewhere between light green and turquoise."

Plate 318

10" Plate (back).

Rare plate, measures full 10".

Plate 319

Creamer.

See Plate 320 on next page. Brown-mottled Fiesta red glaze.

Plate 316

Plate 317

Plate 318

Plate 319

Plate 320

Oddities: Mixing Bowl, Cup, and 7" Plate.

Included is a #4 mixing bowl in a color the owners call "cream of tomato," a cup in Fiesta red with a standard Carnival body and a handle very much like those on the Fiesta cream soup bowl, and a brown-mottled red 7" Fiesta plate. The same glaze can be seen in Plate 312, and several other such pieces have been reported over the years — enough to suggest that HLC may have been toying with the idea of putting it into production, perhaps as competition for a line of dinnerware Stangl made that had a very similar glaze. Stangl's utilized solid turquoise on the inside of the bowls and cups, as well as on the top of the plates, a look HLC could have approximated by pairing the rusty red glaze with turquoise Fiesta.

Plate 321

Demitasse Pot.

This was originally Fiesta red — as you can see inside — but it's now glazed in a copper-bronze luster, and we know of another with silver over its original green. We have photos in our file of a 2-pint jug and an egg cup that both sport silver lustre treatments. Other collectors told us about a dinnerware set they had acquired that they were able to trace back to 1948. It was in cobalt with gold bands and contained 7" plates, dinner plates, 4" fruits, teacups, and a teapot. The company responsible for these lustre applications remains a mystery to us, but there were many small firms in the vicinity of HLC that specialized in decorating ware from the area's several potteries and china companies.

Plate 322

Fruit Bowl.

This Fiesta fruit bowl is Skytone blue; we've never seen another.

Plate 323

Another "Mystery" Piece.

One of a set of three mixing bowls that look for all the world like genuine Fiesta, and they may well be, though opinions of experts differ. The set contains a 6¾" yellow bowl, a 7¾" cobalt bowl, and the 8¾" in red. The bottoms of these bowls are completely glazed and have three sagger pin marks. The band of rings most resemble the footed salad bowl's. Are they Rhead's design that never made it into production? If you have further information, let us hear from you.

Plate 320

Plate 321

Plate 323

Plate 322

Plates 324 – 328
Lamps.

These lamps are made with Fiesta and Harlequin components. The red lamps are both Fiesta. The first one was made from the spherical section and foot of the carafe with the stem of the sweets comport added for the neck. The hole the cord goes through on the bottom is factory glazed. The one on the far right is made of casseroles, a sweets comport stem, and a small fruit bowl as the base. The body of the large cobalt lamp was fabricated from two Harlequin casseroles; once again the neck is a Fiesta sweets comport stem, and the base is a Fiesta fruit bowl. All are excellent examples of what HLC's inventive employees could do given a little time and access to the needed materials! The boudoir lamps made from syrup bottoms (Plates 327 and 328) were more than likely assembled by another company and sold commercially, since there are several in existence and bases are nearly always identical (the marble base is unusual). Both styles are sometimes found with hand-painted flowers. The cobalt Fiesta syrup-lamp has its original shade.

Plate 324

Plate 325

Plate 326

Plate 327

Plate 328

Kitchen Kraft and OvenServe

As early as the 1930s, Homer Laughlin China was the leading manufacturer of a very successful type of oven-to-table kitchenware. These lines were called OvenServe and Kitchen Kraft. They were offered in an extensive assortment of items, patterns, and decals, and today's collectors find them most interesting to research and reassemble into matching sets.

The lovely line with the tulip decals shown in Plate 329 is marked "Kitchen Kraft, OvenServe." In addition to these, expect to find other items — this design turns up every once in awhile, though certainly with less frequency than in years past.

Many floral-decaled Kitchen Kraft lines were produced, every one of them lovely. In Plates 330 through 336, you'll see several.

The label below was found on a floral-embossed spoon and fork set in the rust glaze; examples of this line are shown on page 177.

Plate 329
Casserole in Metal Holder, Cake Plate, Medium Covered Jar, Stacking Refrigerator Set, Salt and Pepper Shakers, and Pie Server.
For a larger listing of available items, see "Suggested Values" in the back of the book.

Guaranteed
To Withstand Changes of

Oven-Dinner Ware
"THE OVEN WARE FOR TABLE SERVICE"

The Homer Laughlin China Co.
Newell, W. Va.

Plate 329

Plate 330
Examples of floral-decaled Kitchen Kraft.

Plate 331
Sun Porch Individual Casserole and Salt and Pepper Shakers.

These choice pieces came out of a New Jersey basement where, covered in soot, they nestled together in a cardboard box stamped "4-Piece Range Set." Unfortunately the box did not survive, but as the picture shows, its 50-year old contents cleaned up to be brand, spanking "old." This time the individual casserole is being used as a drip jar. One of the shakers has been turned around to show the decal on the back.

Plate 332
Sun Porch Tumblers.

Not Kitchen Kraft, of course, but shown here as a point of interest, these tumblers are decorated with a fired-on version of the Sun Porch decal. The matching teapot is on the Century shape and can be seen in Plate 351.

Plate 330

Plate 331

Plate 332

Plates 333 – 334

7" Underplate, Casserole.

Here is an example of the elusive Kitchen Kraft underplate; it matches the casserole in Plate 334. A matching pie plate was recently found with the embossed flowers shown in Plate 338 on its exterior. Another collector reported a pie plate, though with significant differences in the decals. He described a cup and saucer in front of the jug, to its left flowers and a teapot. The lady has nothing in her hands and her hat is a different style, and red and blue, not yellow.

Plate 335

Mixing Bowl, Cake Plate, and Server.

Plate 333

Plate 334

Plate 335

Plate 336

Pie Plate and Platter.

   These are from a line called Kitchen Bouquet, according to the backstamp. It's a favorite of mine, simply because the bright primary colors go so well with Fiesta.

Plates 337 – 340

Custard Set in Wire Rack, 2½-quart Casserole and Underplate, Batter Pitcher, and Ashtray.

   These are examples of the line embossed with the same floral pattern that decorated the handles of the Fiesta Kitchen Kraft spoon, fork, and server. The custard set in the wire rack shows a variety of available colors; yellow and rust are the most commonly encountered, and in addition to those shown, you may also find a piece or two in dark green. The decorative treatment shown in Plate 338 utilizes brightly colored decals over the embossed flowers on the 2½-quart casserole and underplate. The batter pitcher is rare, and white is a hard-to-find color. In Plate 340 is a photo of the standard Kitchen Kraft ashtray. Very few of these have ever been found.

Plate 336

Plate 337

Plate 338

Plate 339

Plate 340

The Kitchen Kraft below is decorated in an Art Deco leaf pattern, one of the Harmony lines we told you about in the chapter entitled "The Story of Fiesta." This line was undiscovered until the sixth edition, and we were doubly excited to learn that a matching line of Kitchen Kraft had been produced. This, of course, is the line that coordinated with red Fiesta.

Plate 341

Casserole, Mixing Bowl, Pie Plate, Spoon, Fork, and Server.

Plate 342

Kitchen Kraft Jar and Nautilus Lug Cereal/Soup Bowl, 6½" and 7½" Plates, Cup and Saucer, Creamer and Sugar Bowl, and Large Vegetable Bowl.

It is interesting to note that collectors report finding several more Nautilus items than those that are listed in the Harmony assortment on page 10.

Plate 343

Nautilus Cup With Fiesta Saucer, Kitchen Kraft Individual Casserole, Nautilus Fruit Bowl and 6½" Plate, 7½" Fiesta Plate, Kitchen Kraft Shakers and Jug With Yellow Lid.

This was designed to go with yellow Fiesta. Collectors have termed this pattern "Shaggy Flower"; it's the decal the company identified as N-1258.

Plate 341

Plate 342

Photo © Adam Anik

Plate 343

Photo © Adam Anik

Children's Sets

Children's dishes were not made in any great amount; they're hard to find, and most collectors are avid in their search for them. You'll find some of these marked with an ink-stamped series of letters and numbers. For help in deciphering these codes, see the section called "Dating Codes and English Measurements."

Plate 344
9" Serving Plate.
    This is unmarked but has all the earmarks of an HLC product. These same comic animal decals may also be found on the shapes used for the Tom and the Butterfly set shown in Plate 348.

Plate 345
Bowl.
    This is decorated with the familiar green and white checks of the Ralston Purina Company; these were made by HLC as premiums for Ralston customers.

Plate 346
Plate, Bowl, and Mug.
    This very exciting set, as you can see, utilizes the Fiesta molds.

Plate 344

Plate 345

Plate 346

180

Plate 347
Dick Tracy Plate, Mug, and Bowl.
   Borrowing a plate from the Century line, this set is rare and very collectible because of the crossover interest in the character collectible field. These are especially sought after, collectors tell us, in California, due to the popularity of collectibles pertaining to the movie industry in that area. On the same mug with a vellum glaze, HLC produced a Little Orphan Annie mug that was offered as a premium by the Ovaltine company.

Plate 348
Tom and the Butterfly Plate, Bowl, and Mug.

Plate 347

Plate 348

Decaled and Striped Century

These are only a few examples of the many different decorations applied to Century shapes. You'll find that many pieces carry the name of the line on the back, and the year of their manufacture is often indicated by a dating code. Some of the more attractive and accessible patterns are being reassembled into sets by today's collectors.

Plate 349

Dinnerware With Stripes.

This is dated 1933/1934, probably made well before the striped Fiesta line. It's the first we've seen. Besides the platters, plates, and teapot shown, the partial set contained bowls in three sizes. Most items were marked with the Wells peacock in silver.

Plate 350

Wells Peacock Trademark.

The Wells family became involved with the company as early as 1889 when William Edwin Wells became Homer Laughlin's partner. Succeeding generations continued as leaders of the firm.

Plate 351

Teapot.

One line, Sun Porch (represented by this teapot and shown also in the chapter on Kitchen Kraft and OvenServe), is novel in that the decal depicts pieces of Fiesta on the table under the umbrella. It is interesting to note that this teapot is the only piece of Sun Porch ever found that is not Kitchen Kraft. There are bowls, a covered jar, a covered jug, a pie plate, an underplate, and a cake plate, but all are Kitchen Kraft. The collector who has them tells us he believes that this is an earlier line than Fiesta and suspects that Rhead may have modeled the carafe and bulb candlesticks after this decal.

Plate 349

Plate 350

Plate 351

Photo © Adam Anik

Plate 352
Dinnerware.

English Garden is the name of this lovely dinnerware. It's dated 1933, and the casserole is marked with the colorful Wells trademark in Plate 350; note the inside decal on the casserole. Also shown are the egg cup; fast-stand gravy boat; plates, 10" and 8"; creamer and sugar bowl; butter dish; syrup jug with lid; and cream soup. Of special interest in this photo is the butter dish. This is actually the Century shape, one of only a few we've ever seen. In virtually every other instance, the one used in decaled lines utilizing Century is the Jade butter dish; you'll see more of this shape on one of the following pages.

Plate 353
6" Plate, Cup and Saucer, Deep Plate, Luncheon Plate, and Fruit Bowl.

For years people with a bit of disdain for inexpensive Depression-era dinnerware have remarked, "They used to give that stuff away at the movies." Well, here is a Century set that really was. Plates with the legend shown have been found in several Northeastern states and at least one in the South. These pieces are never marked on the back, but they are unmistakably HLC.

Plate 352

Plate 353

Photo © Adam Anik

Dogwood

Dogwood is an especially lovely line of HLC dinnerware that was produced in the early 1960s. At least twenty items were made; see "Suggested Values" in the back of the book for a complete listing. Included were five sizes of plates. Among the hard-to-find items in this pattern are the 8" salad plates, the 10" dinner plate, the teapot, and the Kitchen Kraft mixing bowl set. The Dogwood decal has also been reported on Rhythm shapes.

Plate 354
Creamer, Sugar Bowl, and Sauce Boat.

Plate 355
8" Salad Plate, 10" Dinner Plate, Mixing Bowl Set, Teacup and Saucer, Oval Vegetable Bowl, 6" Oatmeal Bowl or 5" Fruit Bowl.
    Note the hard-to-find items previously mentioned.

Plate 354

Plate 355

This very attractive set was made exclusively for Montgomery Ward who offered it for sale in their catalogs from 1944 through 1956. Each piece (thirty-one in all) carries a different design patterned after a Currier and Ives print. The rose-pink decorations suggestive of mulberry historical Staffordshire ware were "printed from fine copper engravings," so states the ad in the 1944 catalog.

These pieces were available: cup and saucer; plates, 10", 8½", 7", 6", and 8" square; dessert/fruit bowl; demitasse cup and saucer; coupe soup; creamer and sugar bowl with lid; sauce boat and stand; egg cup; teapot; oval platters 11", 13", 15"; round platter, 13"; oval vegetable bowl; round vegetable bowls, 8", 9"; and vegetable bowl lid, 9".

Plate 356
(Left to Right) Oval Platters, Cup and Saucer, Sauce Boat and Stand, Sugar Bowl, and Creamer.

VIEW OF HARPER'S FERRY, VA
AN AMERICAN SUBJECT
»> FROM «<
CURRIER & IVES
PRINTS
MADE IN U S A BY
HOMER LAUGHLIN
JAMES PARR ENGRAVER

Plate 356

Historical American Subjects

Produced for the F. W. Woolworth Company who sold it through their retail stores, Historical American Subjects was aptly named. At least nineteen pieces were made, each decorated with a scene reproduced from the original works of Joseph Boggs Beale. All that has been reported to us has been in the rose-pink as shown here except for the 8" plate which has also been found in blue. The line, as far as we know, consisted of plates, 10", 9", 8", and 7"; rim soup, 8½"; dessert/fruit bowl, 5¾"; platters, 13" and 11"; round and oval vegetable bowls, 8¾" and 9½"; cup and saucer; cereal/soup bowl; creamer and sugar bowl; teapot; gravy boat and undertray. Scenes bear titles such as "Betsy Ross and the Flag," "Lincoln's Gettysburg Address," "George Washington Taking Command of the Army," "The First Thanksgiving," and "Paul Revere." Though very hard to find, there's lots of enthusiasm for this line, and prices are already higher than for most decaled dinnerware.

Plate 357
Historical American Subjects Mark.

Plate 358
Various Historical American Subjects Pieces.

Plate 357

Plate 358

Plate 359

La Hacienda Grouping.

La Hacienda is the pattern name; the shape is called Jade. According to the dating code in the backstamp, it was made circa 1935. Though we always thought the stick butter dishes were on the Century shape because they were consistently found in Century-based Mexican lines, here's proof that indeed they belong to the Jade line. Only the round butter dish shown in the Hacienda section and again in Century/English Garden is actually Century.

Plate 360

Unnamed Pattern.

This lovely but unnamed line has a backstamp that indicates a 1933 production date. Note the fast-stand gravy bowl and the 36s bowl directly behind the butter dish. Also shown in the photo is a plate with a Blue Willow decal and a saucer with a courting couple.

Plate 359

Plate 360

Priscilla

This is one of the many beautiful patterns of dinnerware that has become very collectible. It's an extensive line and relatively easy to find. Two styles were produced — the regular line, simple round shapes on Eggshell (their lightweight semiporcelain); and a second line that utilizes the Republic shape. Both are shown below. In addition to the dinnerware, you'll find matching Kitchen Kraft. Among the harder-to-find items are the tall teapot (shape designation unknown) shown in Plate 361 to the far left, the Republic teapot, and these Kitchen Kraft items: the 9½" fruit bowl (far right), coffeepot, and the tab-handled platter. A more complete listing is offered in the "Suggested Values" section. (Note: Other items may be found carrying the same mark but made by Universal China Company; these pieces are generally regarded as desirable enhancements to a Priscilla collection.)

Plate 361
Tall Teapot; Deep Plate, 8½"; Plates, 10" (the second is Republic); Kitchen Kraft Fruit Bowl; Republic Creamer and Sugar Bowl; and Republic Teapot.

Plate 362
Kitchen Kraft Jug; Coffeepot; Mixing Bowls; Casserole; Regular Teapot; and Republic Teapot.

Plate 361

Plate 362

Nautilus

Here's the Nautilus shape again — it was shown in the Mexican lines and again as a basis for two of the Harmony lines. This time the pattern is called Old Curiosity Shop; though very hard to find, it has lots of charm and is popular among HLC dinnerware collectors.

Plate 363
Cup and Saucer, 6½" Plate, Deep Bowl, Casserole With Lid, Fruit Bowl, 11½" Platter, Deep Plate, 9½" Plates, Gravy Boat and Liner, Butter Dish (Jade shape), and Creamer and Sugar Bowl.

Plate 363

Photo © Adam Anik

Decaled Rhythm

Rhythm is a shape designed by Don Schreckengost. We're most familiar with it as one of the colored dinnerware lines, of course, but it was the basis of several decaled lines as well.

Plate 364
Rhythm Rose.
 This is a lovely floral. It was produced from the mid-'40s through the mid-'50s and is marked with the gold stamp: Household Institute, Rhythm Rose.

Plate 364

Plates 365 – 366
American Provincial Pattern.

American Provincial is the name of the pattern in these two plates. Note the variations in the decal as well as the decoration — some items are trimmed with a red stripe while other pieces have gold trim. The salt and pepper shakers are on the Jubilee shape. The large jug has never been reported in the solid colors of Rhythm.

Plate 367
Western Dinnerware.

While we once thought the Western dinnerware was a child's set, we've since heard from a lady who received some as a wedding gift. She tells us that in addition to the place setting, there were serving pieces such as a creamer and sugar bowl, vegetable bowls, and platter. From another source, we've learned that there was even an ashtray to match.

Plate 365

Plate 366

Plate 367

Swing, introduced in 1938, was the first of HLC's shapes in the Eggshell weight. By '45 it was identified only as Eggshell, not to be confused with Eggshell Nautilus, a lighter-weight version of the Nautilus shape, or Eggshell Georgian, a lightweight rendering of a classic English shape. This line was decaled and/or pastel-striped and included a wide variety of pieces allowing for such unusual (for HLC) presentations as a breakfast-in-bed set. The shakers were also used with Virginia Rose and Rhythm. Because of its delicate appearance, pastels and floral treatments abound. And on rare occasions, you may find it in the Hacienda pattern, in blue-trimmed Mexicana, in Conchita, and in Mexicali.

Plate 368
Casseroles.
    These are two lovely floral-decorated casseroles.

Plate 369
Teapot.
    This is the very rare Chinese Green Goddess teapot.

Photo © Adam Anik

Plate 368

Plate 369

Plate 370
After Dinner (or Breakfast-in-Bed) Creamer, Cup and Saucer, and 6" Plate.
   These are in an unnamed floral pattern.

Plate 371
Plate.
   This plate is from an appealing dinnerware line called Colonial Kitchen. On Eggshell Swing you may find a pattern stamped (on the back) Pueblo with a bare-breasted Indian woman making clay pots on a multicolored rug.

Plate 370

Plate 371

Virginia Rose

Virginia Rose was the name given a line of standard HLC shapes which from 1929 until the early 1970s were used as the basis for more than a dozen patterns of decaled or embossed dinnerware. The designer was Fredrick Rhead, and the name was chosen in honor of the daughter of Joseph Mahan Wells, granddaughter of Wm. E. Wells. Virginia Rose was one of the most popular shapes ever produced. Even after it was discontinued for use in the home, the shape was adopted by the hotel china division at HLC and became a bestseller in the field of hotel and institutional ware. Shown here is only a sampling of the many floral patterns you may find on pieces marked Virginia Rose. Among the harder-to-find items are the double egg cup, coffee mug, 8" tray with handles, and the salt and pepper shakers. A matching line of Kitchen Kraft is also available. Some of it is limited as well. The 12" pie plate, salt and pepper shakers, cake plate and server, straight-sided casserole, and the 8" casserole with round sides are scarce. For a more complete listing of available items, see "Suggested Values" in the back of the book.

Plate 372
Plates, 10", 8", 6"; Soups, 8" (one flanged); Salt and Pepper Shakers; Egg Cup; Oatmeal Bowl, 6"; Deep Bowl, 5".

Plate 373
Kitchen Kraft Salt and Pepper Shakers, Casserole, and 8" Tray.
The straight-sided casserole is harder to find than the one shown in Plate 374. The small tray is very scarce and may have been used as an undertray for the casserole.

Plate 372

Plate 373

Plate 374

Kitchen Kraft Covered Casseroles, 8½", 7½"; and Daisy Chain Covered Casserole.

   The casserole on the right is very rare. Like the mugs in Plate 377, the darker decal (the company's JJ-59) indicates 1930s production. This piece is marked DC-714 under the lid and carries the HLC Oven-Serve logo.

Plate 375

Covered Vegetable; Cake Set; Platter, 15"; Plate, 8"; Sauce Boat and Liner; Platter, 9½" ; Butter Dish; Creamer and Sugar Bowl; Cup and Saucer; Kitchen Kraft Casserole, 8".

   This decal was cataloged as UR-128.

Plate 374   Jack and Treva Hamlin Collection

Plate 375

Plate 376
  Water Pitcher, 7½"; Milk Pitcher, 5"; Kitchen Kraft Mixing Bowl Set.

Plate 377
Baltimore Coffee Mugs.
  All are dated 1930; the pattern is JJ-59.

Plate 376

Plate 377

Laughlin Art China

In the early 1900s in an attempt to enter the art pottery field, HLC produced a unique line of art china. It was marked in gold or black with an eagle and the name "Laughlin Art China." Perhaps as many as eighty-nine shapes were used, and several decorating techniques were employed. Most are decaled, but occasionally you will find a hand-decorated piece that may be artist signed. Their most extensive pattern, "Currant," (shown in the following plates) featured brown shaded backgrounds with decals of berries and vines.

Plate 378
Laughlin Art China Mark.

Plate 379
8" Vase With Handles.

Plate 380
7" vase.

Plate 381
2" x 10" Ruffled Salad Bowl, 9½" Plaque, 10" Scalloped Plate.

Plate 378

Plate 379

Plate 380

Plate 381

Plate 382
6½" x 12" "Fe Dora" Bread Tray.

Plate 383
Covered Casserole.

Plate 384
6" Humidor, 6" Bulbous Pitcher, 12" "Orange" Bowl With Handles, and Straight-Sided 6½" Pitcher.

Plate 385
Demitasse or Hot Chocolate Set.

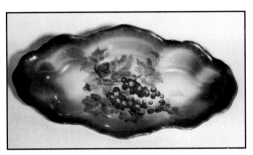

Plate 382

Plate 383

Plate 384

Plate 385

Plate 386
10" Pitcher.
    Called "Dutch Jug" in old company records.

Plate 387
12" Vase.

Plate 388
14" Vase With Handles.

Plate 389
Sugar Baskets.
    The gold-trimmed example is from a line called "Golden Fleece."

Plate 390
9¾", 12", and 16" Vases and Chocolate or After-Dinner Pot.
    Here's another style in an after-dinner pot — it's 10" tall. These items are very rare.

Plate 388

Plate 387

Plate 386

Plate 389

Plate 390

Plates 391 – 394

"White Pets" Line.

   These pieces are hand-painted, though they're probably painted over a decal — as you can see, the same design was used on more than one shape. The vase with the dogs is 8"; the ewer is a magnificent 15½" tall. We have a snapshot in our files of a 7" vase with a swan reflected in water and the tall trumpet-shaped 16" cylinder vase with the same dogs and cattails that you see here. Occasionally, one of these pieces will bear an artist's signature. A small stein has also been reported in this line, and there are sure to be other shapes. The flaking you see in Plate 392 is common to this ware.

Plate 391

Plate 392

Plate 393

Plate 394

A few pieces have been found decorated in Flow Blue with gold trim and decals of children in period costume.

Plate 395
Cup and Saucer.

Plate 396
7", 3-part Candy Dish.

Plate 397
Jardiniere.
This measures a huge 10" x 14½"; with its gold trim and deep color, it's a magnificent example of this type of ware.

Plate 395

Plate 396

Plate 397

Plate 398
Lady's Cuspidor.
This is in Flow Blue with gold trim — it's 5½" x 8½".

Plate 399 – 400
Plates.
Pieces decorated with children are especially desirable.

Plate 398

Plate 399

Plate 400

Plate 401
Large Tankard and Mugs.
    The body of this very rare tankard is the same as those shown in Plates 402 – 404 , but as you can see there are two styles of handles.

Plate 402
Large Tankard.
    This rare item is marked "American Floral."

Plate 403
Large Tankard.
    This item is very rare, especially with the patriotic decal.

Plate 404
Large Tankard and Mugs.
    This tankard has a second portrait on the back; it's very unusual to find a set complete with matching mugs.

Plate 401

Plate 402

Plate 403

Plate 404

Plate 405

Bowl.

One of the most beautiful examples of LAC we've seen, this bowl is unusual in shape as well as subject matter. The lady's breasts are exposed — as far as we know, this has never been seen on a piece from this line before.

Plate 406

Charger.

This matches the tankard shown in Plate 404 and is marked "An American Beauty, Semi-Vitreous China, 1900."

Plate 407

Small Stein.

This one is inscribed "Copyright 1905 by the H.M. Suter Publishing Company"; the name John E. Sheridan is signed on the diagonal near the player's elbow.

Plate 405

Plate 408

Pitcher.

The only example we've ever seen with this fruit decoration.

Plate 409

Small Stein.

This stein was commissioned by a hardware company. It reads "Berger Manufacturing Company Souvenir Mug, Canton, Ohio, Everything in Sheet Metal," on the front, and on the back "Ohio Hardware Association, February 27, 1928." We've also seen these mugs with a multicolored Jacobean design that is very attractive. This shape is probably one of the more commonly found pieces in the assortment.

Plate 406

Plate 407

Plate 408

Plate 409

Dreamland

Children feeding a pet goat, doing laundry, playing badminton and crying when their dog steals the "birdie" decorate this winsome but rare line made by Homer Laughlin in the early years after the turn of the century. It appears to be done in a technique called "pouncing" that was used by several of the larger art pottery manufacturers who operated in the same general area.

Plate 410
Tankard Set.
    A wonderful tankard set on shapes that we have shown before marked Laughlin Art China. Another collector has this set without the brown shading at the bottom, and his is decorated with four different designs.

Plate 411
Vase.
    This tiny vase is a mere 3½".

Plate 412
Ruffled Salad Bowl and Jug.
    This is also an Art China shape. The little jug measures 6½".

Plate 410

Plate 411

Plate 412

Plate 413
10½" Chop/Cake Plate
   Note that the chop/cake plate has closed handles.

Plate 415
16" Vase.

Plate 414 and 417
 Plaques.
   These round plates are shown with two different designs.

Plate 416
10" Vase and 10" Cake Plate.
   Note that this cake plate has open handles.

Plate 413

Plate 414

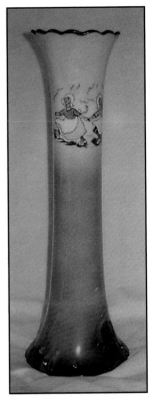

Plate 415

Plate 416

Plate 417

Plate 418

Bowl.

This is a piece from a line marked "Laughlin's Holland." It was referred to by Homer Laughlin as their "orange bowl." This time it's decorated with a scene of three Dutch children watching a mother duck and her ducklings waddle by. This line is extremely rare!

Plate 419

6½" Jug.

Here's another piece from "Laughlin's Holland"; the shape was shown on the previous page in the Dreamland series. This line is extremely rare!

Plates 420 – 422

Unknown Line.

What a shame we've never learned the official name of the line represented here. It's decorated with various scenes of children engaged in outdoor activities, and its shapes are Genesee and Empress. From the provenance provided by the owner, whose mother used these dishes when she was a child, and because we know these two shapes were standard during those years, we date this line 1910–1920.

Plates 423 and 425

Nursery Rhymes Line.

Nursery Rhymes are the theme for this line. The shape is Yellowstone, and these pieces have a family provenance as well. They were given to the owner's mother by her grandfather, a glassblower who worked in many of the glass and pottery houses in the area. The stamp on the back dates this line to 1926. Shown are only three pieces from a nearly complete set.

Plate 418

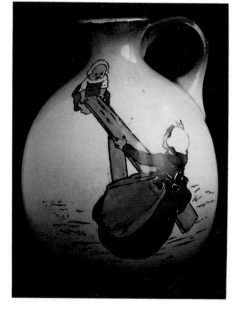

Plate 419

Plate 420

Plate 421

Plate 422

Plate 423

Plate 424

Plate 425

World's Fair: The American Potter

As a tribute to the American Potter, six pottery companies united their efforts and jointly built and operated an actual working kiln at the 1939–1940 World's Fair in New York. A variety of plates, vases, figural items, and bowls were produced and marked with an ink stamp "The American Potter, 1939 (or '40), World's Fair Exhibit, Joint Exhibit of Capital and Labor." The Homer Laughlin China Company entry, designed by Frederick Rhead, is shown in Plate 426. In the center of each plate are the Trylon and Parisphere, adopted symbols of the Fair. These plates have found favor not only with collectors of Homer Laughlin but also with World's Fair enthusiasts, and as a result of the strong Art Deco influence imparted by Rhead into their design, Art Deco aficionados vie to own them too.

Plate 426
Plates.

One of these plates has been found with this commemorative message stamped in gold on the back: "Decorated by Charles Murphy, 150th Anniversary Inauguration of George Washington as First President of the United States, 1789–1939."

Plate 427
Edwin Knowles Marmalade.

Plate 428
Entries From Five Other Companies.

Left to right: Cake set, "Cronin China Co., Minerva, O., National Brotherhood of Operative Potters;" Bowl, "Paden City Pottery, Made in USA," 10"; Plate, "Knowles, Joint Exhibit of Capital and Labor," 10¾"; Marmalade bottom (shown complete with lid in Plate 427), embossed with Trylon and Parisphere and "New York World's Fair," marked Edwin M. Knowles China Co., Semi-Vitreous," 3"; Pitcher, marked "Porcelier Trade Mark, Vitreous Hand Decorated China, Made in U.S.A." The Porcelier pitcher was part of a 7-piece set that included teapots in three sizes, a sugar bowl, a creamer, and a smaller juice pitcher. All of these items are hard to find.

Plate 426

Plate 427

Plate 428

Plate 429
Yellow Vase.
    This is about 7" in height — colossal as these vases go.

Plate 430
Cup and Saucer.
    These are embossed with signs of the Zodiac — they're also rare.

Plate 431
Items Hand Turned at the Fair.
    This variety of small items came in many colors, sizes, and shapes. The Harlequin individual creamer (etched "World's Fair" on the side) measures 2⅛", so you can judge the sizes of the other pieces from that — even the taller vase is under 5". All of these items are rare, especially the bowl and the cobalt candle holder shown on the far right. They all carry an ink stamp, "American Potter."

Plate 429

Plate 430

Plate 431

209

Plate 432

Plates and Ashtray.

These are souvenirs of the Golden Gate International Exposition of 1939 and 1940. They're marked "Golden Gate Intern. Expo., Copyright License 63C, Homer Laughlin, Souvenir," and more than likely, they were designed by Rhead as well.

Plate 433

Four Season Plates.

Each plate measures 4¼" in diameter. Spring shows a man fishing for trout; Summer depicts a family picnicking; a man hunting with his dog represents Autumn; and the Winter plate has a skating scene. These sets are usually found in the colors shown, but a set with all four plates in turquoise has been reported.

Plates 434 and 435

Potter's Plates and Original Box.

Shown are the easiest of the World's Fair items to find. There are two — The Potter at His Wheel and The Artist Decorating the Vase. They've been found in turquoise as shown, light green, and ivory. They're scarce in the latter two colors, and we've seen a couple in tan/mocha shades. One was marked "First Edition For Collectors Limited to 100 Pieces, #85." What is rare, though, is the box these plates came in, shown in Plate 435.

Plates 436 and 437

Pitchers.

Pitchers modeled after the likenesses of George and Martha Washington were popular souvenirs with fairgoers, since 1939 was the 150th anniversary of the inauguration of Washington as the first President of the United States. These are shown in cobalt in Plate 437, though they're rare in that color — most are in ivory. Martha is harder to find than George in any color or style. These are 5" tall, but you'll also find smaller examples that measure about 2". They're sometimes in a bisque finish, and examples in mauve blue and Harlequin yellow have been reported. They may be marked with one or more of these three marks: "The American Potter, New York World's Fair," with the year on a raised disk superimposed over a Trylon; "First Edition For Collectors, New York's World's Fair, 1939"; or "Joint Exhibition of Capital and Labor, American Potter, NY WF, 1939." They were also made as salt and pepper shakers and toothpick holders, but these are generally not marked.

Plate 432

Plate 433

Plate 434

Plate 435

Plate 436

Plate 437

Miscellaneous

Here are a few last items of interest we wanted to share with you.

Plate 438

Sit 'n Sip Set.

Shown with its original carton. These were marketed during the late '60s into the early '70s. Most, though not all, carry advertising messages. You'll often see a similar type of mug set in gift stores today, containing instructions to use the coaster as a lid to keep your coffee hot longer, as may have been the practice then.

Plate 439

Bowl and Mug.

This is from the "other" Tom and Jerry set. But this one's not on Fiesta shapes, so it's not nearly as valuable as the one that is!

Plate 438

Plate 439

Plate 440

Nude Vases and Donkey Ashtray.

Shown glazed in Fiesta red and ivory, one of the vases is marked by hand under the glaze "GAW," more than likely the initials of its creator. All three of these pieces were discovered near Newell, the property of an HLC supervisor. Three more colors have been found — rose, maroon, and spruce. We've seen a photograph of a green donkey ashtray and mauve blue donkey figurine. The owner has two small vases she believes are HLC as well, identical in form (pilgrim flask shapes with angle handles), one in the red and the second in the mauve blue glaze. Both are commemoratives.

Plate 441

Football Trophy.

This was designed by an HLC employee in the early '40s to commemorate Bill Booth, an Ohio State football star from East Liverpool (notice the "O" on his jersey). Booth was tragically killed in an automobile accident, and a very limited number of these trophies were dipped in the Fiesta glazes to present to his teammates. Besides the light green one shown here, a yellow one is on display along with other Fiesta experimental and production pieces at the Homer Laughlin factory, and we have reports of one in ivory and one in spruce green.

Plate 442

Chip 'n Dip Plate.

Though we're not positive, this may well be an HLC product. It measures 12" in diameter and has lots of good characteristics, leading us to suspect that it is. Do you have any information about it?

Plate 440

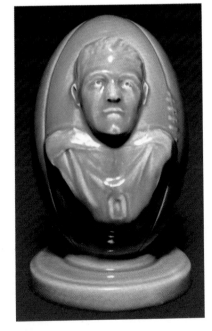

Plate 441

Plate 442

Plate 443

"Leaf Saucers."

Shown in Fiesta red, these were found in the East Liverpool/Newell area by an experienced collector who always thought they were made at HLC although they are unmarked; a saucer in cobalt has been found in the HLC morgue. Made also in green, they are 7" in diameter by ¾" high, a short-production premium go-along for Swanky Swigs.

Plate 444

Doll.

Her name is Delores, marked Marin Tichlana, Made in Spain. She's made of hard plastic and vinyl and stands 15" tall — reminiscent of our Fiesta dancing girl logo.

Plate 445

Neon Clock.

This is contemporary, of course, but wonderful.

Plate 446

Handmade Lamp and Clock.

These go to prove that Fiesta collectors can be just as creative as HLC's employees were when inspired by Fiesta's wonderful colors and shapes.

Plate 444

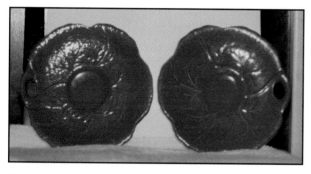

Plate 443

Plate 445

Plate 446

Suggested Values

Values are suggested for items that are in absolutely mint condition — that is to say no chips, "chigger bites," or "dings!" Unless it's a high-quality piece, it will not bring these prices nor should dealers expect it to. The three sagger pin marks that are evident on the underside of many pieces are characteristic and result from the technique employed in stacking the ware for firing. These should in no way be considered damage. Slightly scratched items are usually worth about 30% below "book"; those with heavy scratches or tiny "dings" on areas where the damage is obvious should sell for approximately 50% to 60% below. Chips and hairlines would rapidly accelerate the downward slide. In fact, such damage on a common piece renders it virtually worthless. One should learn to grade merchandise carefully and to adjust prices accordingly. Don't expect to get book price for worn or otherwise inferior items.

Decals when present must be complete, the colors well preserved, with very little wear. When decals are worn, faded, or otherwise appear to be in less-than-mint condition, items should be evaluated following the above guidelines.

When buying odd lids and bases, remember that glaze colors vary, and some lids and openings will be just enough off-round that they will not properly fit together. If you do buy them separately, expect to pay 50% to 60% of listed values for lids and 40% to 50% for bases. For example, if a sugar bowl is listed at $20.00, its lid would be approximately $10.00 to $12.00 and its base $8.00 to $10.00.

Fiesta
See Plates 1 through 52.

The first column of figures represents the range of values suggested for these colors: red, cobalt and ivory. The second column contains values for turquoise (with exceptions), yellow, and light green. Collectors report that items discontinued in 1946 are generally harder to find in turquoise, since that color was not introduced until mid-1937, an entire year after the other colors. In the column on the far left, you'll notice that some of the items in the listing are followed by asterisks. These are the ones we mentioned that were dropped in 1946. To evaluate these items in turquoise, use the first column of values (for red, cobalt, and ivory), generally the high end; for all other turquoise pieces, use the second column. The third column offers a range of values for the Fifties colors — chartreuse, dark green, rose, and gray. This is the first survey where not a single person suggested that any of these colors were preferred over the others. While rose and gray were on top for awhile, our previous survey indicated a possibility that dark green and chartreuse were becoming the more popular colors. Watch the market in your area. Such preferences may be regional, though home-decorating magazines indicate that we'll soon be seeing chartreuse used to accent earth tones. You'll see that values in the column for medium green continue to soar. At the recommendation of our advisors, we increased these ranges from as little as 20% to as much as 50%. The last column, "As Specified," contains values for the specific colors listed on the far left.

Unless this is the first of our books you've purchased, I'm sure you know by now, that our evaluations are based on a nationwide survey of some of the country's most prestigious dealers and collectors. This time, as always, we found opinions to be widely varied, and as we struggled to reconcile their differences and make a semblance of order from the chaos, it became obvious to us that even after almost twenty-five years, values have not yet leveled off — in fact, there is nothing to suggest that a plateau is even in sight. Prices for items under $50.00 showed little change, but the higher-end accessory pieces and anything in medium green took some amazing jumps! (Now I understand the incredulous look I used to see on my 90-year-old father's face when I would tell him the price of his medication, a good cigar, or sliced bread, for that matter! Bob and I had our "go" at Fiesta in its infancy — $7.00 for a pair of 12" cobalt vases, $3.25 for my yellow syrup pitcher, $40.00 for a red covered onion soup.) Remember, we're no longer collectors, nor are we dealers, so we have nothing to gain by manipulating the outcome of our survey. We purposely shuffle the reports that have been sent in so we have no idea whose estimate we're reading. All of our respondents are seasoned dealers/collectors, and we have faith in each of them. But anyone who has been in the antiques and collectibles field very long knows that the market always has two strata: those who can sell at high book or above, depending on their clientele, location, charisma, etc., while others find it impossible to get those prices and are more apt to concentrate on turning their merchandise over more quickly. I respect both. Then there are the collectors; some can pay the top dollar, many can't. We would be amiss to represent only one aspect of the market; we're trying to find a median. So following the methods we've always used, we threw out the high and low estimates and averaged the others. Figures were never rounded off more than two dollars in either direction. What we arrived at we feel represents a high average. Please keep in mind that when we say "high average" we mean that in most parts of the country, these might very likely be the "asking" prices of dealers who specialize, carry a large stock, and sell only quality merchandise. As we all know, if we're willing to expend the effort to seek them out, there are always bargains to be had from other, less convenient resources. Dealers, we're not trying to set your prices, and you may have to adjust them up or down according to what the market will bear in your area or selling arena.

Suggested Values

The values we suggest for anything $500.00 and up should probably be regarded as minimum. It is impossible to set an accurate price range, even with the help of the advanced collectors and dealers who took part in our survey. Some of these items are so rare, even these veterans will seldom, if ever, have them in stock or see them on the market. When these rarities do come up for sale, they will naturally go to the bidder with the highest offer.

There are fine points to collecting and price assessing that must be left up to the collector, since much of it is a matter of individual preference. Some collectors search out the medium green individual salad bowls that have no inside rings and the medium green cups that do and are willing to pay a premium to get them. Others find the issue to be of little consequence. So because a price guide can be only a general interpretation of the market, we'll leave those fine points up to the individual, though we have tried to make you aware of the fact that those subtle variations exist.

We invite you to let us hear from you with your viewpoints, new finds, or about any new trends and developments. You may also write or call us with questions, which we will be happy to answer if we can. Our address is 1202 Seventh St., Covington, Indiana 47932. Our phone number is (765) 793-2392; FAX: (765) 793-2249.

NEV = No Established Values

	Red, Cobalt, Ivory	Yellow, Turquoise, Lt. Green	1950s Colors	Med. Green	As Specified
Ashtray	50.00 – 60.00	42.00 – 47.00	78.00 – 88.00	160.00 – 180.00	
Bowl, covered onion soup					
cobalt and ivory					650.00 – 725.00
red					675.00 – 750.00
turquoise[1]					3,000.00+
yellow & lt. green					550.00 – 600.00
Bowl, cream soup	50.00 – 60.00	38.00 – 42.00	65.00 – 72.00	4,000.00+	
Bowl, dessert; 6"	48.00 – 52.00	32.00 – 38.00	45.00 – 52.00	450.00 – 475.00	
Bowl, footed salad*	325.00 – 350.00	270.00 – 300.00			
Bowl, fruit; 11¾"*	260.00 – 300.00	225.00 – 265.00			
Bowl, fruit; 4¾"	28.00 – 35.00	22.00 – 28.00	30.00 – 40.00	425.00 – 485.00	
Bowl, fruit; 5½"	28.00 – 35.00	22.00 – 28.00	32.00 – 40.00	65.00 – 75.00	
Bowl, individual salad, 7½"					
red, turquoise, or yellow				95.00 – 105.00	75.00 – 85.00
Bowl, mixing; #1*[2]	190.00 – 225.00	155.00 – 170.00			
Bowl, mixing; #2*[2]	110.00 – 125.00	90.00 – 110.00			
Bowl, mixing; #3*[2]	115.00 – 130.00	100.00 – 120.00			
Bowl, mixing; #4*[2]	135.00 – 155.00	120.00 – 130.00			
Bowl, mixing; #5*[2]	155.00 – 185.00	140.00 – 155.00			
Bowl, mixing; #6*[2]	220.00 – 265.00	180.00 – 200.00			
Bowl, mixing; #7*[2]	275.00 – 350.00	260.00 – 280.00			
Bowl, nappy, 8½"*	50.00 – 60.00	35.00 – 40.00	55.00 – 62.00	120.00 – 140.00	
Bowl, nappy, 9½"*	55.00 – 65.00	48.00 – 52.00			
Bowl, unlisted salad;					
yellow					90.00 – 105.00
ivory, red, or cobalt*[3]					450.00 – 500.00
Candle holders, bulb; pr*	120.00 – 130.00	85.00 – 95.00			
Candle holders, tripod; pr*	550.00 – 600.00	430.00 – 465.00			
Carafe*	260.00 – 300.00	200.00 – 250.00			

[1] Reported mail bid sale: $4,000.00.

[2] Please keep in mind that these values are for mixing bowls in absolutely mint condition — no nicks inside or out.

[3] Though this is our average, we thought it prudent to tell you that two of our advisors suggested values in the four-figure range — a good example of what the high-end market will bear.

	Red, Cobalt, Ivory	Yellow, Turquoise, Lt. Green	1950s Colors	Med. Green	As Specified
Casserole	175.00 – 200.00	125.00 – 150.00	275.00 – 300.00	675.00 – 725.00	
Casserole, French;					
yellow					250.00 – 300.00
other standard color[4]					625.00 – 650.00
Casserole, promo.;					
complete, standard color[5,]					135.00 – 150.00
Coffeepot	225.00 – 245.00	175.00 – 195.00	325.00 – 350.00		
gray					410.00 – 430.00
Coffeepot, demitasse*[6]	410.00 – 435.00	320.00 – 340.00			
Comport, 12"*	170.00 – 185.00	135.00 – 148.00			
Comport, sweets*	80.00 – 90.00	65.00 – 75.00			
Creamer	25.00 – 35.00	18.00 – 22.00	35.00 – 40.00	70.00 – 80.00	
Creamer, ind.; in red					225.00 – 250.00
turquoise & cobalt					325.00 – 345.00
yellow					60.00 – 70.00
Creamer, stick-handled*	60.00 – 70.00	40.00 – 45.00			
Cup, demitasse	65.00 – 75.00	55.00 – 65.00	325.00 – 350.00		
Cup, see teacup					
Egg cup	65.00 – 70.00	52.00 – 58.00	150.00 – 160.00		
Lid, mixing bowls, #1 – 3					
any color					750.00 – 785.00
Lid, mixing bowl #4					
any color					1,000.00+
Lid, mixing bowls #5 – 6	NEV				
Marmalade*	260.00 – 285.00	215.00 – 230.00			
Mug, Tom and Jerry	78.00 – 85.00	50.00 – 60.00	85.00 – 100.00	100.00 – 125.00	
Mustard*	235.00 – 250.00	185.00 – 200.00			
Pitcher, disk juice;					
gray[7]					2,500.00+
red					425.00 – 450.00
yellow					35.00 – 45.00
Harlequin yellow					52.00 – 62.00
celadon green					200.00 – 225.00
any other color[8]	NEV				
Pitcher, disk water	150.00 – 165.00	100.00 – 125.00	260.00 – 275.00	1,150.00+	
Pitcher, ice*	135.00 – 160.00	110.00 – 140.00			
Pitcher, 2-pt. jug	100.00 – 120.00	70.00 – 90.00	125.00 – 150.00		
Plate, cake*[9]	860.00 – 885.00	730.00 – 755.00			
Plate, calendar; 1954, 10"					40.00 – 45.00
1955, 9"					45.00 – 50.00
1955, 10"					40.00 – 45.00
Plate, chop; 13"	45.00 – 55.00	35.00 – 40.00	80.00 – 100.00	250.00 – 275.00	
15"	65.00 – 75.00	42.00 – 48.00	100.00 – 115.00		
Plate, compartment; 10½"	35.00 – 40.00	35.00 – 40.00	65.00 – 75.00		
12"[10]	50.00 – 60.00	45.00 – 55.00			

[4] Two in our survey recommended values of $1,000.00 for these, and a mail bid for a cobalt bottom realized $1,900.00.

[5] These have been reported in Harlequin yellow, maroon, and spruce; these colors are rare and will command much higher prices (E-bay sale: $425.00).

[6] Values suggested for turquoise were as high as $550.00 and $600.00.

[7] One recently sold at mail bid for $4,000.00; another went for the asking price of $3,000.00.

[8] One in turquoise recently exceeded a minimum mail bid of $10,000.

[9] These are average prices as reported, but one person reported selling a red cake plate for $1,800.00.

[10] None has ever been reported in turquoise. In that color, value not established.

	Red, Cobalt, Ivory	Yellow, Turquoise, Lt. Green	1950s Colors	Med. Green	As Specified
Plate, deep	50.00 – 60.00	35.00 – 40.00	50.00 – 55.00	110.00 – 120.00	
Plate, 6"	5.00 – 7 .00	4.00 – 5.00	7.00 – 9.00	15.00 – 20.00	
Plate, 7"	8.00 – 10.00	7.00 – 9 .00	10.00 – 13.00	28.00 – 32.00	
Plate, 9"	14.00 – 18.00	9.00 – 12.00	18.00 – 22.00	40.00 – 45.00	
Plate, 10"	35.00 – 40.00	28.00 – 32.00	48.00 – 52.00	95.00 – 110.00	
Platter	40.00 – 45.00	30.00 – 35.00	52.00 – 58.00	120.00 – 140.00	
Salt & pepper shakers, pr.	25.00 – 30.00	18.00 – 22.00	40.00 – 45.00	120.00 – 140.00	
Sauce boat	65.00 – 75.00	40.00 – 45.00	72.00 – 78.00	140.00 – 155.00	
Saucer	4.00 – 5.00	3.00 – 4.00	5.00 – 6.00	10.00 – 12.00	
Saucer, demitasse	18.00 – 22.00	15.00 – 18.00	85.00 – 95.00		
Sugar bowl with lid	50.00 – 55.00	40.00 – 45.00	65.00 – 72.00	150.00 – 160.00	
Sugar bowl, ind.;					
in turquoise					335.00 – 350.00
in yellow					110.00 – 120.00
Syrup *[11]	360.00 – 400.00	300.00 – 325.00			
Teacup	30.00 – 35.00	20.00 – 25.00	32.00 – 38.00	52.00 – 58.00	
Teapot, large *	200.00 – 220.00	165.00 – 185.00			
Teapot, medium	175.00 – 200.00	140.00 – 165.00	290.00 – 325.00	1,000.00+	
Tom and Jerry bowl					
ivory w/gold letters					240.00 – 260.00
Tom and Jerry mug					
ivory w/gold letters					55.00 – 65.00
Tom and Jerry bowl,					
not on Fiesta mold[12]					50.00 – 60.00
Tom and Jerry mug,					
not on Fiesta mold[12]					10.00 – 15.00
Tray, figure-8; cobalt					75.00 – 90.00
turquoise or yellow					275.00 – 350.00
Tray, relish *					
Center insert	50.00 – 55.00	38.00 – 42.00			
Side insert	42.00 – 48.00	35.00 – 40.00			
Relish base	80.00 – 85.00	60.00 – 65.00			
Tray, relish; gold decorated					220.00 – 250.00
Tray, utility *	38.00 – 42.00	32.00 – 38.00			
Tumbler, juice;	40.00 – 45.00	35.00 – 40.00			
rose					60.00 – 65.00
chartreuse,					
Harlequin yellow,					
dark green[13]					440.00 – 460.00
Jubilee colors except gray					100.00 – 125.00
gray					250.00+
maroon	NEV				
Tumbler, water*	70.00 – 85.00	55.00 – 60.00			
Vase, bud*	90.00 – 110.00	70.00 – 80.00			
Vase, 8"*[14]	600.00 – 700.00	535.00 – 600.00			
Vase, 10"*[14]	780.00 – 850.00	700.00 – 750.00			
Vase, 12"*[14]	1,200.00+	1,000.00+			

[11] Badly faded lids will detract from value.

[12] See Plate 439.

[13] Recently brought $1,000.00 each.

[14] Some feel color is not significant in evaluating the large vases.

Fiesta Ironstone
See Plate 53.

Use the high side of the range to evaluate red Ironstone.

Ashtray, rare	25.00 – 30.00
Coffee mug	22.00 – 26.00
Coffee server	70.00 – 78.00
Covered casserole	50.00 – 60.00
Creamer	5.00 – 7.00
Egg cup	8.00 – 12.00
Fruit, small	5.00 – 7.00
Marmalade	45.00 – 55.00
Nappy, large	15.00 – 20.00
Pitcher, disk water	55.00 – 65.00
Plate, 7"	3.00 – 4.00
Plate, 10"	7.00 – 9.00
Platter, 13"	18.00 – 22.00
Salad bowl, 10"	45.00 – 50.00
Salt & pepper shakers, pr.	10.00 – 14.00
Sauce boat	25.00 – 30.00
Sauce boat stand.	35.00 – 40.00
in red.	120.00 – 135.00
Saucer	1.50 – 2.00
Soup/cereal	7.00 – 9.00
Soup plate	10.00 – 14.00
Sugar bowl with lid	12.00 – 16.00
Teacup	4.00 – 6.00
Teapot, medium	55.00 – 65.00

Fiesta Kitchen Kraft
See Plates 54 through 66.

Use the high side of the range to evaluate red and cobalt. Note: See Jubilee and Rhythm sections for information concerning the value of mixing bowls in the colors of those lines.

Bowl, mixing, 6"	65.00 – 75.00
Bowl, mixing, 8"	82.00 – 92.00
Bowl, mixing, 10"	100.00 – 120.00
Cake plate	55.00 – 65.00
Cake server	130.00 – 140.00
Casserole, individual	140.00 – 155.00
Casserole, 7½"	85.00 – 90.00
Casserole, 8½"	100.00 – 110.00
Covered jar, large	300.00 – 320.00
Covered jar, medium	260.00 – 280.00
Covered jar, small	270.00 – 290.00
Covered jug	250.00 – 275.00
Fork	100.00 – 125.00
Metal frame for platter	22.00 – 26.00
Pie plate, 9"	40.00 – 45.00
with advertising in gold	55.00 – 65.00
Pie plate, 10"	40.00 – 45.00
in spruce green	270.00 – 290.00
Platter	68.00 – 78.00
in spruce green	325.00 – 350.00
Salt & pepper shakers, pr.	95.00 – 105.00
Spoon	100.00 – 125.00
Spoon, ivory, 12"	500.00+
Stacking refrigerator lid	70.00 – 80.00
in ivory	190.00 – 205.00
Stacking refrigerator unit	45.00 – 55.00
in ivory	180.00 – 195.00
Underplate	NEV

Fiesta Casuals
See Plates 67 and 68.

Because yellow Carnation is reported to be harder to find than Hawaiian Daisy, some collectors feel it should be worth 25% more than suggested values. This is a matter of personal preference.

Plate, 7"	8.00 – 10.00
Plate, 10"	10.00 – 15.00
Platter, oval	35.00 – 40.00
Saucer	5.00 – 6.00

Fiesta with Stripes and/or Decals
See Plates 69 through 81.

Even after many surveys and pricing updates, there is still a wide range of opinions concerning how to evaluate striped Fiesta. Using red, ivory, and cobalt Fiesta prices as a basis, some felt it should be of equal value, one says 50% higher, and another thinks it should be three to five times as much. With this in mind, you be the judge!

As for decaled items, opinions ranged from 20% less than red, ivory, and cobalt up to 100% more. Decaled Fiesta is in short supply and market values are obviously hard to analyze. All of the following are Fiesta with the turkey decal:

Plate, 9½"..................................95.00 – 105.00	Plate, chop, 13".....................................110.00 – 135.00
Plate, cake; KK ....180.00 – 200.00	Plate, chop, 15".....................................165.00 – 190.00

New Fiesta
See Plates 82 through 101.

Aside from a few pieces we evaluated in the text, we feel that suggesting secondary market prices at this time would be premature and irresponsible on our part.

Harlequin
See Plates 102 through 123.

The response we got from Harlequin collectors this time seemed to indicate a heightened interest in the line and an increased understanding of rarities, color preferences, and market activity. So we're branching out and expanding the pricing structure for the first time, especially in the area of medium green. We're breaking ground, so to speak, and since these ideas are comparatively new, please bear with us. Relatively few contributed this information, since all of it was a "write-in" (as they couldn't just "fill in the blanks" over last year's book), so if you beg to differ with us, please do so. But we felt that there was enough input from a sufficient number of collectors (obviously very avid and knowledgeable) to warrant its inclusion in this edition. As you'll see, reported sales often were much higher than the price survey recommended. Hopefully with the next edition, we can zero in on the median range with more accuracy.

Use the high side of the range to evaluate maroon, dark green, gray, and spruce green. Medium green Harlequin is even more scarce than medium green Fiesta, and as seasoned collectors vie with each other for these rarities, prices are soaring. Based on this activity, values are suggested individually for many medium green items; when no specific value is given, we suggest that you at least double the upper side of the high range. Colors represented by the lower end of the high range are chartreuse, rose, red, light green, and mauve blue. Those items marked with an asterisk are rare or non-existent in light green; no market value has been established for them.

NEV = No Established Value.

	Low Range	High Range	As Specified	Sales Price Report
Ashtray, basketweave	30.00 – 35.00	52.00 – 58.00		
Ashtray, regular*	32.00 – 38.00	48.00 – 53.00		
Ashtray, saucer*	45.00 – 50.00	55.00 – 63.00		
ivory			90.00 – 115.00	

	Low Range	High Range	As Specified	Sales Price Report
Bowl, cream soup	18.00 – 22.00	25.00 – 30.00		
medium green			600.00+	
Bowl, fruit, 5½"	6.00 – 8.00	8.00 – 11.00		
medium green			25.00 – 35.00	
Bowl, individual salad	22.00 – 28.00	36.00 – 42.00		
medium green			50.00 – 75.00	
Bowl, mixing; Kitchen Kraft, 6"				
red or light green			80.00 – 90.00	
Bowl, mixing; Kitchen Kraft, 8"				
mauve blue			100.00 – 125.00	
Bowl, mixing; Kitchen Kraft, 10"				
yellow			100.00 – 125.00	
Bowl, nappy, 9"	22.00 – 26.00	35.00 – 40.00		
medium green			75.00 – 95.00	
Bowl, oval baker	22.00 – 27.00	35.00 – 40.00		
Bowl, 36s	22.00 – 26.00	35.00 – 40.00		
spruce green or maroon			70.00 – 82.00	
medium green			90.00 – 115.00	
Bowl, 36s oatmeal	12.00 – 16.00	22.00 – 26.00		
medium green			30.00 – 45.00	
Butter dish, 1/2-lb.	90.00 – 115.00	120.00 – 135.00		
cobalt			250.00 – 300.00	
Candle holders, pr.*	220.00 – 240.00	260.00 – 285.00		
Casserole	80.00 – 95.00	145.00 – 160.00		
medium green[15]			350.00 – 450.00	
Creamer, high-lip; any color			120.00 – 130.00	
Creamer, individual*	16.00 – 20.00	30.00 – 35.00		
Creamer, novelty	24.00 – 28.00	35.00 – 40.00		
medium green[16]	NEV			950.00
Creamer, regular	10.00 – 14.00	15.00 – 20.00		
medium green			40.00 – 50.00	
Cup, demitasse	38.00 – 42.00	90.00 – 110.00		
medium green			225.00 – 275.00	
Cup, large (Epicure body)				
medium green	NEV			
any other color			160.00 – 180.00	
Egg cup, double	15.00 – 20.00	25.00 – 28.00		
medium green	NEV			350.00
Egg cup, single*	20.00 – 25.00	30.00 – 35.00		
Marmalade*[18]	185.00 – 200.00	210.00 – 240.00		
Nut dish, basketweave[19]	10.00 – 13.00	15.00 – 18.00		
Perfume bottle, any color			100.00 – 120.00	
Pitcher, service water	65.00 – 70.00	90.00 – 105.00		
medium green	NEV			800.00 – 2,000.00
Pitcher, 22-oz. jug	35.00 – 40.00	62.00 – 68.00		
medium green			250.00+	300.00
Plate, deep	15.00 – 20.00	25.00 – 30.00		
medium green			70.00 – 75.00	

[15] Opinions varied widely on our survey with prices up to double this amount suggested.

[16] One known to exist.

[18] You may find spruce, maroon, rose, and mauve the higher priced colors for this item.

[19] Expect to pay more for light green and rose. One of the original Japanese nut cups sold on E-bay recently for about $170.00.

	Low Range	High Range	As Specified	Sales Price Report
Plate, 6"	3.00 – 4.00	4.00 – 5.50		
Plate, 7"	5.00 – 6.00	6.00 – 8.00		
Plate, 9"	8.00 – 10.00	12.00 – 14.00		
Plate, 10"	20.00 – 24.00	32.00 – 36.00		
medium green			80.00 – 100.00	
Platter, 11"	15.00 – 18.00	20.00 – 25.00		
medium green			150.00 – 200.00	
Platter, 13"	18.00 – 22.00	28.00 – 32.00		
medium green			200.00 – 250.00	
Relish tray, mixed colors*			280.00 – 300.00	
Salt & pepper shakers, pr.	15.00 – 18.00	22.00 – 26.00		
medium green			150.00+	250.00
Sauce boat	18.00 – 22.00	30.00 – 35.00		
medium green			100.00+	225.00
Saucer	1.00 – 2.00	3.00 – 4.00		
Saucer, demitasse	10.00 – 15.00	22.00 – 28.00		
medium green			125.00+	200.00
Sugar bowl with lid	15.00 – 20.00	28.00 – 32.00		
medium green			100.00+	150.00
Syrup*, in red or yellow			175.00 – 200.00	
spruce or mauve			250.00 – 300.00	
Teacup	7.00 – 9.00	9.00 – 11.00		
Teapot	80.00 – 85.00	120.00 – 145.00		
medium green (very rare)	NEV			
Tumbler	40.00 – 45.00	52.00 – 58.00		
Tumbler with car decal			60.00 – 65.00	

Harlequin Animals
See Plates 124 through 129.

Any animal in a standard color ....150.00 – 175.00

Any animal in a non-standard color ....250.00 – 275.00

Mavericks, near to full-size with gold..........45.00 – 55.00

smaller, of porcelain-type material ....22.00 – 28.00

Riviera and Ivory Century
See Plates 130 through 153.

NEV = No Established Value.

Batter set, standard colors........................260.00 – 285.00

with decals.....................................160.00 – 170.00

red ....NEV

ivory, with covered sugar bowl
& 11½" square platter ....NEV

Bowl, baker, 9" ....22.00 – 28.00

Bowl, cream soup; with liner, ivory ....70.00 – 75.00

Liner only...20.00 – 25.00

Bowl, fruit; 5½" ....10.00 – 12.00

cobalt ....30.00 – 35.00

Bowl, nappy, 7¼" ....22.00 – 28.00

Bowl, oatmeal; 6" ....35.00 – 40.00

Bowl, utility, ivory ....45.00 – 50.00

Butter dish, ¼-lb.......................................125.00 – 135.00

turquoise ....270.00 – 290.00

cobalt..240.00 – 250.00

Butter dish, ½-lb, other Riviera colors ....90.00 – 120.00

cobalt, ½-lb ....250.00 – 300.00

Casserole ....85.00 – 110.00

Creamer...10.00 – 12.00

Cup & saucer, demi; ivory ....70.00 – 80.00

Jug, covered ....120.00 – 130.00

Jug, open..85.00 – 95.00

Jug, open, 4½", ivory..NEV

Pitcher, juice; yellow ....110.00 – 120.00
Pitcher, juice; mauve blue ....190.00 – 210.00
Plate, compartment ....NEV
Plate, deep ....20.00 – 24.00
Plate, 6"..6.00 – 8.00
Plate, 7"..9.00 – 12.00
     cobalt...25.00 – 35.00
Plate, 9"..15.00 – 18.00
Plate, 10"..50.00 – 55.00
Platter, 11½"..20.00 – 25.00
Platter, 11¼", closed handles.....................22.00 – 28.00
Platter, 12", cobalt ....65.00 – 70.00
Platter, 15"..50.00 – 60.00

Salt & pepper shakers, pr. ....15.00 – 20.00
Sauce boat...22.00 – 27.00
Sauce boat, fast-stand ....75.00 – 85.00
Saucer ....3.00 – 4.00
Sugar bowl with lid ....15.00 – 20.00
Syrup with lid...145.00 – 160.00
Teacup ....8.00 – 11.00
Teapot...135.00 – 145.00
Tidbit, 2-tier, ivory ....70.00 – 75.00
Tumbler, handled..70.00 – 75.00
     ivory ....135.00 – 145.00
     (These have been reported in spruce green, NEV)
Tumbler, juice..48.00 – 52.00

Amberstone
See Plates 154 through 158.

NEV = No Established Value.
Items marked with an asterisk (*) are decorated with the black Amberstone pattern.

Ashtray, rare ....25.00 – 30.00
Bowl, jumbo salad..38.00 – 42.00
Bowl, soup/cereal...5.00 – 8.00
Bowl, vegetable...12.00 – 16.00
Butter dish*...35.00 – 45.00
Casserole...50.00 – 55.00
Coffee server ....52.00 – 58.00
Covered jam jar..45.00 – 50.00
Covered mustard ....55.00 – 60.00
Creamer..6.50 – 7.50
Cup & saucer*..6.00 – 8.00
Deep soup, 8"*...10.00 – 12.00
Dessert dish...5.00 – 7.00
Jumbo mug, none as yet found.....................NEV

Pie plate*...32.00 – 38.00
Pitcher, disk water ....50.00 – 60.00
Plate, bread & butter*......................................2.50 – 3.50
Plate, salad*...3.00 – 4.50
Plate, 10"*...6.00 – 8.00
Platter, oval*..12.00 – 16.00
Platter, round serving*...................................15.00 – 20.00
Relish tray, center handle*..............................25.00 – 30.00
Salt & pepper shakers, pr. ....12.00 – 14.00
Sauce boat..18.00 – 22.00
Sauce boat stand ....20.00 – 24.00
Sugar bowl with lid ....7.00 – 8.50
Tea server ....48.00 – 52.00

Casualstone
See Plate 159.

NEV = No Established Value.
Items marked with an asterisk (*) are decorated with the gold Casualstone pattern.

Ashtray, rare ....12.00 – 15.00
Bowl, jumbo salad; 10" ....35.00 – 38.00
Bowl, round vegetable..................................12.00 – 15.00
Bowl, soup/cereal..4.00 – 6.00
Butter dish, stick*...32.00 – 38.00
Casserole...40.00 – 45.00
Coffee server ....40.00 – 45.00
Creamer..4.00 – 5.00

Cup & saucer*..6.00 – 8.00
Deep plate*..7.00 – 8.50
Dessert ....4.50 – 5.50
Jumbo mug..12.00 – 18.00
Marmalade ....40.00 – 45.00
Pie plate*...24.00 – 28.00
Pitcher, disk type ....40.00 – 45.00
Plate, bread & butter*......................................2.50 – 3.50

Plate, dinner*	6.00 – 8.00
Plate, salad*	3.50 – 4.50
Platter, oval, 13"*	12.00 – 15.00
Platter, round*	12.00 – 15.00
Relish tray*	15.00 – 18.00

Salt & pepper shakers, pr.	7.00 – 8.50
Sauce boat	13.00 – 17.00
Sugar bowl with lid	7.00 – 8.50
Tea server	25.00 – 30.00

Carnival
See Plates 160 and 161.

Use the low range of values for these colors: gray, light green, yellow, and dark green. The high side represents values for cobalt, red, ivory, and turquoise.

Fruit, small	5.00 – 7.00
Oatmeal 35s	4.00 – 6.00
Plate, 6½"	2.00 – 3.00

Saucer	1.00 – 2.00
Teacup	4.00 – 6.00

Epicure
See Plates 162 and 163.

Bowl, cereal/soup	25.00 – 30.00
Bowl, covered vegetable	65.00 – 75.00
Bowl, fruit	18.00 – 22.00
Bowl, nappy, 8¾"	30.00 – 35.00
Casserole, individual	75.00 – 80.00
Coffeepot, 10"	125.00 – 150.00
Creamer	15.00 – 20.00
Gravy bowl	35.00 – 40.00
Ladle, 5½"	45.00 – 50.00
Nut dish, 4"	30.00 – 35.00

Pickle (small oval platter)	35.00 – 40.00
Plate, 6½"	7.00 – 9.00
Plate, 8"	18.00 – 22.00
Plate, 10"	30.00 – 35.00
Platter, large	28.00 – 32.00
Salt & pepper shakers, pr.	20.00 – 25.00
Sugar bowl with lid	25.00 – 30.00
Teacup & saucer	20.00 – 25.00
2-tier tidbit	60.00 – 65.00

Jubilee
See Plates 164 through 167.

After years of confusion, we now realize that the only gray 10" mixing bowl known to man came from one of the Jubilee 3-piece bowl sets. There are no gray 6" or 8" bowls. (See page 230 for value of price list in Plate 166.)

NEV = No Established Value.

Bowl, cereal/soup	6.00 – 8.00
Bowl, fruit	4.00 – 5.00
Bowl, mixing; KK, 6"	90.00 – 110.00
Bowl, mixing; KK, 8"	100.00 – 115.00
Bowl, mixing; KK, 10"	120.00 – 140.00
gray	NEV
Bowl, nappy, 8½"	7.00 – 9.00
Casserole	35.00 – 40.00

Coffeepot	40.00 – 45.00
Creamer	5.00 – 6.50
Cup & saucer	4.00 – 6.50
Cup & saucer, AD	12.00 – 15.00
Egg cup	7.00 – 11.00
Fiesta juice tumbler	100.00 – 125.00
Fiesta juice pitcher, celadon green	200.00 – 225.00
gray	2,500.00+

Plate, 6"...1.50 – 2.50
Plate, 7"...3.00 – 4.50
Plate, 9"...5.00 – 7.00
Plate, 10"..8.00 – 10.00
Plate, calendar; cream, 1953.....................20.00 – 25.00
Plate, chop ....14.00 – 17.00

Platter, 11"..8.00 – 10.00
Platter, 13"..9.00 – 12.00
Salt & pepper shakers, pr. ....6.00 – 9.00
Sauce boat..9.00 – 12.00
Sugar bowl with lid ....7.00 – 10.00
Teapot...40.00 – 45.00

Skytone/Suntone
See Plates 168 through 170.

Use values for Jubilee to price these lines.

Pastel Nautilus
See Plates 171 through 173.

Bowl, cream soup..9.00 – 11.00
Bowl, flat soup (deep plate)...............................7.00 – 10.00
Bowl, footed oatmeal; 6".....................................6.00 – 8.50
Bowl, fruit; 5"...5.00 – 6.50
Bowl, tab-handled soup/cereal.........................8.00 – 10.00
Bowl, oval vegetable..9.00 – 12.00
Bowl, round nappy ....9.00 – 12.00
Casserole with lid...38.00 – 42.00
Creamer ....7.00 – 8.50
Cup & saucer ....10.00 – 12.00
Cup & saucer, AD; NEV
(Can anyone verify the existence of this item?)

Egg cup, double. ....12.00 – 15.00
Gravy boat ....12.00 – 15.00
Plate, 6"...2.50 – 3.50
Plate, 7"...5.00 – 6.50
Plate, 8"...5.00 – 6.50
Plate, 9"...6.00 – 8.00
Plate, 10"...9.00 – 12.00
Platter, 13"..12.00 – 15.00
Platter, 11"..9.00 – 12.00
Platter/gravy boat liner, 9" ....9.00 – 12.00
Sugar bowl with lid ....10.00 – 14.00

Rhythm
See Plates 174 through 183.

Bowl, footed cereal/chowder.........................9.00 – 13.00
   brown, black, cobalt, or white ....18.00 – 22.00
Bowl, fruit; 5½"...5.00 – 6.50
Bowl, mixing; KK, 6"..90.00 – 110.00
Bowl, mixing; KK, 8"......................................100.00 – 115.00
Bowl, mixing; KK, 10" ....125.00 – 145.00
Bowl, nappy ....8.00 – 12.00
Bowl, salad; large...45.00 – 55.00
Bowl, soup...8.00 – 10.00
Casserole lid...45.00 – 55.00
      (bottom is nappy)
Creamer, 2¾"...6.00 – 8.00
Cup & saucer..8.00 – 11.00
Cup & saucer, AD; scarce...............................150.00 – 200.00
Plate, 6"..5.00 – 6.00
Plate, 7"..6.00 – 8.00
Plate, 8", very rare..15.00 – 18.00
Plate, 9"..7.00 – 10.00

Plate, 10"...10.00 – 13.00
Plate, calendar..9.00 – 13.00
Plate, snack...22.00 – 28.00
   maroon..95.00 – 110.00
Platter, 11½"...12.00 – 14.00
Platter, 13½"...14.00 – 16.00
Salt & pepper shakers, pr. ....9.00 – 12.00
Sauce boat..10.00 – 15.00
   cobalt..18.00 – 22.00
Sauce boat stand ....10.00 – 14.00
Spoon rest, colors other than white, turquoise,
   or dark green ....185.00 – 200.00
   white...110.00 – 125.00
   dark green..275.00 – 325.00
   turquoise...325.00 – 375.00
Sugar bowl with lid ....12.00 – 16.00
Teapot...45.00 – 50.00
3-tier tidbit ....35.00 – 40.00

Serenade
See Plates 184 through 188.

Bowl, fruit .... 7.00 – 11.00	Plate, 9" .... 9.00 – 12.00
Bowl, lug soup .... 22.00 – 26.00	Plate, 10" .... 15.00 – 20.00
Bowl, nappy, 9" .... 20.00 – 25.00	Plate, chop .... 22.00 – 28.00
Casserole .... 65.00 – 75.00	Plate, deep .... 22.00 – 28.00
Casserole base, Kitchen Kraft .... 30.00 – 40.00	Platter, 12½" .... 15.00 – 20.00
Matching lid .... 65.00 – 72.00	Salt & pepper shakers, pr. .... 14.00 – 18.00
Complete .... 100.00 – 115.00	Sauce boat .... 18.00 – 22.00
Creamer .... 12.00 – 18.00	Sugar bowl with lid .... 15.00 – 20.00
Pickle dish .... 15.00 – 20.00	Teacup & saucer .... 12.00 – 15.00
Plate, 6" .... 4.00 – 5.00	Teapot .... 85.00 – 100.00
Plate, 7" .... 5.00 – 7.00	

Tango
See Plate 189.

Use the high side of the range to evaluate red, spruce green, and maroon items.

Bowl, fruit; 5¾" .... 5.00 – 6.50	Plate, 9" .... 6.00 – 8.00
Bowl, nappy, 8¾" .... 9.00 – 12.00	Plate, 10" .... 9.00 – 11.00
Bowl, oval baker, 9" .... 9.00 – 12.00	Plate, deep .... 8.00 – 11.00
Casserole .... 40.00 – 50.00	Platter, 11¾" .... 9.00 – 12.00
Creamer .... 6.00 – 8.00	Salt & pepper shakers, pr. .... 10.00 – 12.00
Cup & saucer .... 7.00 – 9.00	Saucer .... 1.50 – 2.50
Plate, 6" .... 3.00 – 4.00	Sugar bowl with lid .... 8.00 – 10.00
Plate, 7" .... 3.00 – 4.50	

Wells Art Glaze
See Plates 190 through 197.

Batter set, 3-pc. .... 175.00 – 200.00	Pickle dish with handles .... 18.00 – 24.00
Bowl, cream soup .... 22.00 – 28.00	Plate, 6" .... 6.00 – 8.00
Bowl, fruit; 5" .... 10.00 – 13.00	Plate, 7" .... 9.00 – 12.00
Bowl, nappy, 8" .... 18.00 – 24.00	Plate, 9" .... 12.00 – 16.00
Bowl, oatmeal 36s .... 18.00 – 24.00	Plate, 10" .... 20.00 – 25.00
Bowl, oval baker, 9" .... 18.00 – 24.00	Plate, chop; with handles .... 20.00 – 25.00
Casserole .... 62.00 – 68.00	Plate, deep .... 16.00 – 20.00
Coffeepot, individual .... 100.00 – 120.00	Plate, square, 6" .... 12.00 – 15.00
Covered jug, 9" .... 110.00 – 125.00	Platter, oval, 11½" .... 20.00 – 25.00
Covered jug, with decals .... 62.00 – 72.00	Platter, oval, 13½" .... 25.00 – 30.00
Covered muffin .... 60.00 – 68.00	Platter, oval, 15½". .... 32.00 – 37.00
Cream soup stand .... 12.00 – 16.00	Sauce boat .... 20.00 – 25.00
Creamer .... 18.00 – 22.00	Sauce boat, fast-stand .... 28.00 – 32.00
Creamer, individual .... 15.00 – 20.00	Sauce boat liner with handles .... 15.00 – 20.00
Cup, bouillon; with handles .... 18.00 – 22.00	Sugar bowl, individual, open .... 12.00 – 15.00
Cup, coffee; 4¾" .... 15.00 – 20.00	Sugar bowl with lid. .... 18.00 – 22.00
Cup & saucer .... 15.00 – 20.00	Syrup .... 90.00 – 115.00
Cup & saucer, AD .... 25.00 – 30.00	Syrup, with decals .... 50.00 – 60.00
Egg cup, double .... 18.00 – 22.00	Teapot, Empress, rare .... 200.00 – 300.00
Nut dish/butter pat .... 12.00 – 14.00	Teapot, regular .... 80.00 – 90.00

Orange Tree Bowls
See Plates 198 and 199.

Add 10% for colors other than turquoise.

Set of five ....200.00 – 235.00

Mexican Decaled Lines
Mexicana, Hacienda, Conchita, and Max-i-cana
See Plates 201 through 222.

To simplify the problem of evaluating these lines, we have compiled a general listing that basically will apply to the first three patterns mentioned above (on Century shapes) and Max-i-cana on Yellowstone. Not all of these items have been found in every pattern. Letter codes have been used to indicate pieces that so far are known to exist in only the coded patterns: H — Hacienda; Me — Mexicana; Ma — Max-i-cana. Remember that prices given below are for pieces with mint decals. Examples with worn or scratched decals are worth no more than chipped ones.

Bell (H)..85.00 – 95.00
Bowl, baker, 9".................................28.00 – 32.00
Bowl, cream soup; rare (H, Ma) ....60.00 – 68.00
Bowl, deep, 2½" x 5" (Me) ....40.00 – 44.00
Bowl, fruit; 5"...................................12.00 – 14.00
Bowl, lug soup; 4½" (Ma, Me)...........35.00 – 40.00
Bowl, oatmeal; 6".............................25.00 – 30.00
Bowl, vegetable; 8½"........................25.00 – 30.00
Bowl, vegetable; 9½"........................28.00 – 32.00
Butter dish, ½-lb. (H, Ma)..............125.00 – 140.00
    round (H) ....220.00 – 235.00
Casserole.......................................120.00 – 135.00
Creamer..15.00 – 20.00
Creamer, large (Ma) ....22.00 – 26.00
Cup & saucer.....................................18.00 – 22.00
Egg cup, rolled edge (Me, Ma).............40.00 – 45.00
Egg cup, torpedo shape (Me, Ma) ....32.00 – 38.00
Plate, 6"...5.00 – 7.00
Plate, 7"..12.00 – 14.00

Plate 9"..18.00 – 22.00
Plate, 9½" (10")................................38.00 – 44.00
Plate, deep, 8"...................................22.00 – 25.00
Platter, 10".......................................30.00 – 34.00
Platter, oval or square well, 11½" ....32.00 – 38.00
Platter, oval or square well, 13½".........45.00 – 50.00
Platter, square well, 15".....................45.00 – 50.00
Sauce boat..30.00 – 35.00
Sauce boat liner (Me, Ma) ....28.00 – 32.00
Sugar bowl with lid ....28.00 – 32.00
Sugar bowl, large (Ma) ....28.00 – 33.00
Syrup jug, covered, Century (H, Me)*......375.00 – 425.00
Tall covered jug, Century, (H, Me)* ....425.00 – 475.00
Teapot, rare (H, Me) ....140.00 – 160.00
Tumbler, fired-on design, 6-oz............10.00 – 13.00
Tumbler, fired-on design, 8-oz............14.00 – 17.00
Tumbler, fired-on design, 10-oz...........15.00 – 20.00
    *Jugs with missing lids are worth one-third to one-half as much as those with lids.

Kitchen Kraft Conchita and Mexicana
See Plates 203, 218 through 220.

Bowl, mixing; 6".................................28.00 – 32.00
Bowl, mixing; 8".................................32.00 – 37.00
Bowl, mixing; 10"...............................42.00 – 46.00
Cake plate, 10½".................................32.00 – 37.00
Cake server.......................................60.00 – 70.00
Casserole, individual ....85.00 – 95.00
Casserole, 7½"....................................78.00 – 83.00
Casserole, 8½"....................................75.00 – 80.00
    OvenServe, Handy Andy.................50.00 – 60.00
    Metal base ....15.00 – 20.00
Covered jar, large ....150.00 – 160.00

Covered jar, medium ....120.00 – 135.00
Covered jar, small...........................120.00 – 130.00
Covered jug....................................155.00 – 170.00
Fork...65.00 – 70.00
Pie plate ....30.00 – 35.00
Refrigerator stack unit.......................42.00 – 46.00
    Lid ....50.00 – 55.00
Salt & pepper shakers, pr. ....50.00 – 55.00
Spoon..65.00 – 70.00
Underplate, 9"...................................35.00 – 40.00
Underplate, 6" (rare)..........................40.00 – 45.00

Max-i-cana Fiesta

See Plate 221.

This line is so rare that even very advanced collectors tell us they've never seen a piece.

Cup & saucer	40.00 – 50.00	Plate, 6"	14.00 – 17.00
Fruit, 5½"	35.00 – 40.00	Plate, 10"	40.00 – 45.00
Nappy, 8½"	45.00 – 55.00	Platter	50.00 – 60.00

Miscellaneous Mexican Lines

See Plates 222 through 227.

After carefully studying the results of our survey, we found very little difference between the average of the values suggested for "Mexicana, Hacienda, and Conchita" and the values offered for the less-familiar lines such as Max-i-cana Yellowstone and Mexicali Virginia Rose. So in order to simplify this section of the price guide, we suggest that for any Mexican decal on any shape other than Century — Swing, Nautilus, Virginia Rose, Liberty, and Harlequin are shown in this issue — use the "Mexicana, Hacienda, Conchita" values, placing the top of the value range for the miscellaneous lines at its low end (for the flat pieces) to about the middle range (for the molded hollow ware). The harder-to-find items such as the butter dish, egg cup, and casserole, for instance, will bring just as much in one Mexican decaled line as another.

Go-Alongs

See Plates 228 through 261.

NEV = No Established Value.

Plate 228:	Pitcher with fired on Mexican figures	38.00 – 42.00
	Tumbler	10.00 – 14.00
Plate 229:	Coaster set	15.00 – 18.00
	Napkin ring, each	5.00 – 7.00
	Placecard holder, each	5.00 – 7.00
	Tumbler with raffia wrap & enameled cactus	10.00 – 14.00
Plate 230:	Tumbler or sherbet	12.00 – 15.00
Plate 231:	Rattan tumbler holders, each	15.00 – 18.00
Page 232:	Metal frame for Fiesta jam set (cream soup)	70.00 – 85.00
	Metal frame for Fiesta marmalade, very rare	80.00 – 100.00
	Metal frame for Fiesta chop plate	45.00 – 55.00
Plate 233:	Metal frame for Fiesta salad service set, very rare	100.00 – 125.00
Not shown:	Metal frame for Fiesta mustard & marmalade	80.00 – 90.00
	Metal frame for Fiesta cake plate	40.00 – 45.00
	Metal revolving base for Fiesta relish tray	32.00 – 36.00
Shown in artist's rendering:	Metal frame for Fiesta promotional casserole	35.00 – 40.00
	Metal frame for Fiesta condiment set (mustard and shakers), very rare	80.00 – 95.00
	Metal frame for Fiesta double tidbit set with folding stand	100.00 – 125.00

Plate 234: Fiesta 3-tier tidbit tray (in mixed colors)..90.00 – 100.00
(Add 10% for each plate in red or cobalt — 20% for each plate in the '50s colors)

Plate 235: Metal holder for Harlequin tumbler..22.00 – 24.00

Plate 236: Harlequin nut dish..40.00 – 50.00

Plate 237: Century nut dish in ivory..50.00 – 60.00

Plate 238: Century 2-tier tidbit tray in ivory..60.00 – 70.00

Plate 239: Hankscraft egg cup..6.00 – 8.00
Hankscraft egg poacher with glass insert...50.00 – 60.00

Plate 240: Metal popcorn set, 5-pc., excellent paint..90.00 – 100.00

Plate 241: Frame for Fiesta ice-lip pitcher & tumblers (watch for repros)..............................80.00 – 95.00

Plate 242: Metal holder for Fiesta nappy...16.00 – 20.00
Metal dripolator insert for Fiesta teapot..12.00 – 18.00
Metal frame for Fiesta jam set..70.00 – 80.00
Wireware holder for Fiesta juice set...60.00 – 75.00
Sta Bright Flatware, 3-pc. setting..9.00 – 13.00
Fiestawood tray with glass insert..100.00 – 110.00

Not shown: Metal holder for Kitchen Kraft platter...20.00 – 25.00
Metal holder for Kitchen Kraft pie plate..18.00 – 23.00
Metal holder for Kitchen Kraft casserole...18.00 – 23.00

Plate 243: Insert for Fiestawood tray...15.00 – 20.00

Plate 245: Metal 3-part tidbit set, excellent paint...62.00 – 72.00

Plate 246: Cabinet...NEV

Plate 247: Fiestawood salad bowl..85.00 – 90.00

Plate 248: Fiestawood salad bowl..85.00 – 90.00

Plate 249: Wooden tray/metal base for Fiesta chop plate...65.00 – 70.00

Plate 250: Fiestawood hors d'oeuvres tray...85.00 – 90.00

Plate 251: Metal handle for Fiesta mixing bowl-ice bucket...50.00 – 65.00

Plate 252: Fiestawood hors d'oeuvres tray...85.00 – 90.00

Plate 253: Sheet of decals...60.00 – 70.00

Plate 254: Wastebasket..50.00 – 60.00

Plate 255: Metal Kitchenware bread box...55.00 – 65.00
Metal Kitchenware garbage can...75.00 – 85.00

Plate 256: Metal Kitchenware bread box...55.00 – 65.00

Plate 257: Metal Kitchenware canister set, 4-pc. ....95.00 – 105.00
Metal Kitchenware napkin holder ....45.00 – 55.00

Not shown: Metal Kitchenware stool ....100.00 – 110.00
Metal Kitchenware 3-tier vegetable bin ....75.00 – 82.00

Plate 258: Quikut flatware set, mint in box ....80.00 – 90.00

Plate 259: Japan tea set: pot, sugar & creamer, 6 plates, 6 cups & saucers ....75.00 – 100.00

Plate 260: Tablecloth & napkin set ....25.00 – 30.00

Plate 261: Ash stand ....100.00 – 125.00

Not shown: Luncheon set, tablecloth & 4 napkins, circa 1930s-'40s, color & design compatible ....25.00 – 45.00

Commercial Adaptations and Ephemera
See Plates 262 through 289.

Plate 262: Fiesta price lists, 1930s through 1940s ....65.00 – 75.00
1940s through 1950s ....45.00 – 55.00
1950s on ....40.00 – 48.00

Plate 263: Epicure price list ....85.00 – 95.00

Plate 265: Riviera price list ....85.00 – 95.00

Plate 266: Fiesta Kitchen Kraft price list ....75.00 – 95.00

Plate 267: Harlequin price list ....70.00 – 85.00

Not shown: Ads from 1960s ....30.00 – 35.00

Jubilee price list (see Plate 166) ....25.00 – 35.00

Plate 268: Fiesta store display, complete, NM ....1,000.00 – 1,400.00

Plate 269: Fiesta carton for dinnerware set..80.00 – 90.00

Plate 270: Fiesta carton (no dancing girl logo) ....28.00 – 32.00

Not shown: Fiesta carton for juice set (no dancing girl logo) ....30.00 – 35.00

Plate 271: Fiesta carton, dancing girl logo, small to large..35.00 – 45.00

Plate 272 and Plate 273: Fiesta Ensemble display ad...125.00 – 135.00

Plate 274: Fiesta ashtray, commemorative or advertising..60.00 – 70.00

Plate 275: Kitchen Kraft pie plate with advertising ....65.00 – 75.00
In spruce green ....275.00 – 300.00

Plate 276: Fiesta fruit bowl, Lazarus Anniversary ....35.00 – 40.00

Plate 277:   Fiesta plate, Lazarus Anniversary ....40.00 – 50.00

Plate 278:   Fiesta egg cup, Lazarus Anniversary ....50.00 – 60.00

Plate 279:   Fiesta tumbler, Lazarus Anniversary ....65.00 – 70.00

Plate 280:   Fiesta syrup with Dutchess tea..90.00 – 105.00

Plate 281:   Soup can label (watch for repros) ....8.00 – 10.00

Plate 282:   National Dairy Council punch-outs, as shown (watch for repros)........................120.00 – 130.00

Plate 283:   Fiesta on Homemaker's Recipe File ....12.00 – 15.00

Plate 284:   Riviera on corn package..8.00 – 12.00

Plate 285:   Fiesta Tom & Jerry mugs in white (or color inside), 1-color advertising ....38.00 – 42.00
             2-color advertising...45.00 – 50.00
             3-color advertising...50.00 – 60.00
             4-color advertising...58.00 – 68.00
             Fiesta Tom & Jerry mugs in color with advertising ....70.00 – 80.00
             Fiesta Tom & Jerry mugs, color inside, no advertising..28.00 – 32.00
             Matching Sit n' Sip coasters ....25.00 – 30.00

Plate 286:   Buick Sit n' Sip coasters ....25.00 – 30.00

Plate 287:   Buick Tom & Jerry mugs ....70.00 – 75.00

Plate 288:   Buick ashtray...70.00 – 75.00

Plate 289:   New Fiesta mug...4.00 – 5.00

The Morgue; Experimental
See Plates 298 through 328.

Because most of the items shown in these chapters are one of a kind or at least extremely rare, market values have not been established. The maroon mug in Plate 311 is one from a set of fifteen which along with a large bowl was dipped at the factory as a special gift for a supervisor. The average suggested price on our survey was $1,000.00 to $1,200.00. One estimate was several hundred dollars higher, and prices exceeding $8,000.00 were suggested for the ivory individual teapot, French casserole, and footed mixing bowl.

Lamps, Plates 324 through 328

Fiesta lamp with fabricated body ....400.00 – 450.00
Harlequin lamp with fabricated body......325.00 – 375.00
Syrup lamp base, undecorated ....240.00 – 260.00

Syrup lamp base, hand painted ....250.00 – 270.00
    with original shade, add ....30.00 – 35.00

Kitchen Kraft and OvenServe
See Plates 328 through 336.

Use the higher side to evaluate the more collectible lines such as Sun Porch, Kitchen Bouquet, etc.

Bowl, mixing; 6"................................20.00 – 24.00	Covered jar, small..60.00 – 70.00
Bowl, mixing; 8"................................20.00 – 25.00	Covered jug...85.00 – 95.00
Bowl, mixing; 10"..............................30.00 – 35.00	Pie plate..32.00 – 38.00
Cake plate..30.00 – 35.00	Platter...38.00 – 42.00
Cake server......................................35.00 – 42.00	Metal base ....20.00 – 25.00
Casserole, individual ....50.00 – 60.00	Salt and pepper shakers, pr........................38.00 – 42.00
Casserole, 6".....................................35.00 – 40.00	Spoon..35.00 – 40.00
Casserole, 8½"...................................35.00 – 42.00	Stacking refrigerator lid.............................28.00 – 33.00
Metal base ....15.00 – 20.00	Stacking refrigerator unit...........................25.00 – 30.00
Covered jar, large............................100.00 – 110.00	Underplate ....18.00 – 22.00
Covered jar, medium.........................80.00 – 90.00	

Embossed Line
See Plates 337 through 340.

Add 50% when decals are present.

Ashtray ....30.00 – 40.00	Bowl, tab-handled soup; 7"...........................9.00 – 10.00
Batter pitcher...................................55.00 – 65.00	Casserole, 6"...10.00 – 12.00
Bean pot, 4x4½"................................10.00 – 12.00	Casserole, 7½"...20.00 – 25.00
Bean pot, 4¼x5½"..............................10.00 – 12.00	Casserole, 8½"...25.00 – 30.00
Bowl, 4"...4.00 – 5.50	Casserole, 10"..32.00 – 38.00
Bowl, fruit; 5½" ....8.00 – 10.00	Cup, 3¾", rare ....15.00 – 18.00
Bowl, mixing; 6¼"................................9.00 – 12.00	Custard cup, 3½"...4.00 – 5.00
Bowl, mixing; 7¼"..............................12.00 – 15.00	Pie plate, 9" ....16.00 – 20.00
Bowl, mixing; 8½"..............................16.00 – 20.00	Plate, 7"..5.00 – 7.00
Bowl, oval baker, 6½" ....7.00 – 8.50	Plate, 10"..8.00 – 10.00
Bowl, oval baker, 8½" ....10.00 – 12.00	Platter, deep, oval, 8" ....10.00 – 12.00
Bowl, oval baker, 11"..........................15.00 – 20.00	Platter, deep, oval, 12" ....14.00 – 16.00
Bowl, ramekin, handled, 4½" ....5.00 – 6.00	Saucer, 5¾" ....1.50 – 2.00

Harmony Lines
See Plates 341 through 343.

For Kitchen Kraft items not listed here, use the high side of the range of values suggested for Kitchen Kraft above.

Bowl, cereal/soup ....12.00 – 14.00	Cup & saucer...8.00 – 12.00
Bowl, fruit, 5½" ....6.00 – 8.00	Fork, KK..45.00 – 50.00
Bowl, mixing; KK, 10"..........................30.00 – 35.00	Pie plate, KK, 10".......................................30.00 – 35.00
Bowl, nappy, 9".................................15.00 – 18.00	Plate, 6" ....3.00 – 4.00
Bowl, oval baker, 10".........................16.00 – 22.00	Plate, 7" ....6.00 – 9.00
Cake server, KK................................45.00 – 50.00	Plate, 9" ....9.00 – 12.00
Casserole, KK, 8"...............................40.00 – 45.00	Spoon, KK..45.00 – 50.00

Children's Sets
See Plates 344 through 348.

Plate 344: Serving plate, 9"...35.00 – 40.00

Plate 345: Ralston bowl ....35.00 – 40.00

Plate 346: Animal Characters on Fiesta shapes, set ....500.00 – 550.00
　　　　　On shapes other than Fiesta, set...120.00 – 140.00

Plate 347: Dick Tracy set
　　　　　Plate ....100.00 – 125.00
　　　　　Soup/cereal ....100.00 – 135.00
　　　　　Mug...100.00 – 135.00

Plate 348: Tom & the Butterfly set
　　　　　Plate ....40.00 – 50.00
　　　　　Bowl...50.00 – 65.00
　　　　　Mug..50.00 – 65.00

Decaled and Striped Century
See Plates 349 through 353.

Because it is impossible to list every Century-based dinnerware line produced by HLC, we offer these suggestions to help you determine approximately how much you should expect to pay for the following:

1) For place-setting items (plates, cups and saucers, small bowls, etc.) purchased one at a time in a very simple pattern, use Carnival prices.
2) For place-setting items purchased one at a time in a more desirable pattern (for example, Sun Porch, English Garden, etc.), use 50% of Mexicana prices.
3) For larger serving pieces or purchases of larger lots of a very simple pattern, use 50% of Mexicana prices.
4) For larger serving pieces or purchases of larger lots of a more desirable pattern, use 75% of Mexicana prices.

Dogwood
See Plates 354 through 355.

Values are given for pieces with excellent gold trim.

Bowl, cereal; 6"............................10.00 – 12.00		Plate, 7"....................................10.00 – 12.00
Bowl, fruit, 5¾".............................6.00 – 8.00		Plate, 8", scarce.........................12.00 – 15.00
Bowl, mixing; KK, 6½".................35.00 – 45.00		Plate, 9".......................................8.00 – 10.00
Bowl, mixing; KK, 8¾".................35.00 – 45.00		Plate, 10", scarce.......................12.00 – 15.00
Bowl, mixing; KK, 10½"...............35.00 – 45.00		Platter, 11¾"..............................20.00 – 25.00
Bowl, oval vegetable, 9½"............20.00 – 25.00		Platter, 13½"..............................25.00 – 35.00
Bowl, round vegetable, 8¾".........20.00 – 25.00		Sauce boat.................................20.00 – 28.00
Bowl, soup; 8"............................12.00 – 15.00		Sauce boat liner, 8½"................25.00 – 30.00
Creamer......................................12.00 – 15.00		Sugar bowl with lid...................10.00 – 12.00
Cup & saucer.............................10.00 – 12.00		Teapot..75.00 – 85.00
Plate, 6"..4.00 – 5.00		

Americana
See Plate 356.

Bowl, coupe soup	12.00 – 15.00	Plate, 7"	5.00 – 7.00
Bowl, cream soup	60.00 – 75.00	Plate, 8" square	12.00 – 15.00
Bowl, dessert/fruit	6.00 – 9.00	Plate, 8½"	12.00 – 15.00
Bowl, oval vegetable, 8½"	20.00 – 25.00	Plate, 10"	20.00 – 28.00
Bowl, round vegetable, 8"	20.00 – 25.00	Platter, 11"	15.00 – 20.00
Bowl, round vegetable, 9"	20.00 – 25.00	Platter, 13"	20.00 – 25.00
Bowl lid, 9"	35.00 – 45.00	Platter, 15"	50.00 – 55.00
Creamer	12.00 – 15.00	Platter, round, 13"	35.00 – 40.00
Cup & saucer	12.00 – 15.00	Sauce boat	12.00 – 15.00
Cup & saucer, AD	25.00 – 30.00	Sauce boat stand	45.00 – 60.00
Egg cup	15.00 – 25.00	Sugar bowl with lid	18.00 – 25.00
Plate, 6"	3.00 – 4.00	Teapot	80.00 – 100.00

Historical American Subjects
See Plates 357 and 358.

To evaluate this line, use suggested prices for Americana.

Jade
See Plates 359 and 360.

Values for decaled Jade may be computed by using the suggestions under "Decaled and Striped Century."

Priscilla
See Plates 361 and 362.

Reports from dealers are that Priscilla sells well for them. This line was also made by Universal China; theirs are marked like HLC's, and Priscilla aficionados find that these pieces add dimension to their collections. Values are given for pieces with excellent gold trim.

Bowl, fruit, 5"	7.00 – 8.00	Pitcher, water; KK	30.00 – 35.00
Bowl, fruit; KK, 9½", scarce	32.00 – 38.00	Plate, 6"	6.00 – 7.00
Bowl, mixing; small, KK, 6"	35.00 – 40.00	Plate, 7"	8.00 – 10.00
Bowl, mixing; medium, KK, 8"	35.00 – 40.00	Plate, 8"	9.00 – 10.00
Bowl, mixing; large, KK, 10"	35.00 – 40.00	Plate, 9"	9.00 – 10.00
Bowl, oval vegetable, 9"	20.00 – 25.00	Plate, 10"	12.00 – 15.00
Bowl, round vegetable, 8"	20.00 – 25.00	Platter, tab-handled, made by Universal	25.00 – 30.00
Bowl, soup, 8"	12.00 – 15.00	Platter, 9"	20.00 – 25.00
Cake plate, KK, 11"	20.00 – 25.00	Platter, 13½"	25.00 – 30.00
Casserole, round, KK, 8½"	35.00 – 40.00	Sauce boat	20.00 – 25.00
Coffeepot, KK	85.00 – 95.00	Sugar bowl with lid	20.00 – 25.00
Creamer	15.00 – 20.00	Teapot, regular	80.00 – 90.00
Cup & saucer	12.00 – 15.00	Teapot, Republic, hard to find	80.00 – 90.00
Pie plate, KK, 9½"	25.00 – 30.00	Teapot, tall, hard to find, made by Universal	80.00 – 90.00

Nautilus
See Plate 363.

Values for decaled Nautilus (other than Harmony) may be computed by using the suggestions under "Decaled and Striped Century."

Decaled Rhythm
See Plates 364 through 367.

Plate 364:   Rhythm Rose

Bowl, mixing; KK, small	12.00 – 15.00
Bowl, mixing; KK, medium	15.00 – 18.00
Bowl, mixing; KK, large	20.00 – 25.00
Cake plate, KK, 10½"	18.00 – 22.00
Cake server, KK	35.00 – 40.00
Casserole, KK, 8½"	35.00 – 40.00
Coffeepot, KK	35.00 – 40.00
Creamer	7.00 – 9.00
Cup & saucer, AD	15.00 – 18.00
Pie plate, KK, 9½"	18.00 – 20.00
Pitcher, jug type, KK	35.00 – 40.00
Plate, 6"	3.00 – 5.00
Plate, 9"	7.00 – 9.00
Plate, deep, 8"	12.00 – 14.00
Platter, 13"	15.00 – 18.00
Sauce boat	12.00 – 14.00
Sugar bowl with lid	12.00 – 14.00
Underplate, KK, 6"	10.00 – 12.00
Underplate, KK, 9"	12.00 – 15.00

Plates 365 – 366: American Provincial Spoon rest .... 100.00 – 125.00
Use the Rhythm Rose prices to evaluate other American Provincial.

Plate 367:   Western

Bowl, fruit	12.00 – 15.00
Bowl, vegetable	15.00 – 20.00
Cup & saucer	15.00 – 18.00
Plate, 9"	15.00 – 18.00

Swing
See Plates 368 through 371.

NEV = No Established Value

Plate 369: Green Goddess teapot, very rare .... NEV
     Values for other pieces of Swing dinnerware lines may be computed by using the suggestions under "Decaled and Striped Century."

Virginia Rose
See Plates 372 through 377.

NEV = No Established Value. Values are given for pieces with excellent gold or silver trim.

Bowl, covered vegetable; 9"	100.00 – 125.00
Bowl, deep, 5"	18.00 – 22.00
Bowl, fruit; 5½"	5.00 – 8.00
Bowl, mixing; KK, 6"	35.00 – 45.00
Bowl, mixing; KK, 8"	35.00 – 45.00
Bowl, mixing; KK, 10"	35.00 – 45.00
Bowl, oatmeal; 6"	12.00 – 15.00
Bowl, oval vegetable; 8", scarce	30.00 – 35.00
Bowl, oval vegetable; 9"	20.00 – 25.00
Bowl, oval vegetable; 10"	28.00 – 32.00
Bowl, vegetable; 7½", scarce	28.00 – 32.00
Bowl, vegetable; 8½"	22.00 – 28.00
Bowl, vegetable; 9½"	30.00 – 35.00
Butter dish, ½-lb.	125.00 – 175.00
Cake plate, KK, scarce	60.00 – 70.00
Cake server, KK, scarce	60.00 – 75.00
Casserole, Daisy Chain, DC–714	NEV
Casserole, KK, OvenServe:	
Round sides, 8", scarce	80.00 – 100.00
Straight sides, scarce	150.00 – 175.00
Creamer	15.00 – 20.00
Cup & saucer	12.00 – 15.00
Egg cup, double	60.00 – 75.00
Mug, coffee	50.00 – 65.00
Pie plate, KK, 9½"	28.00 – 35.00
Pie plate, KK, large, scarce	35.00 – 40.00
Pitcher, milk; 5"	65.00 – 80.00
Pitcher, water; 7½"	150.00 – 175.00
Plate, 6"	7.00 – 8.00
Plate, 7"	11.00 – 14.00
Plate, 8", scarce	15.00 – 18.00
Plate, 9"	8.00 – 10.00
Plate, 10"	12.00 – 15.00
Plate, deep; 1" flange	15.00 – 20.00
Plate, deep; no flange	15.00 – 20.00
Platter/gravy liner, 9"	28.00 – 32.00
Platter, 10½", scarce	30.00 – 35.00
Platter, 11½"	20.00 – 25.00
Platter, 13"	28.00 – 35.00
Platter, 15½"	40.00 – 50.00
Salt & pepper shakers:	
KK, scarce, pr.	150.00 – 175.00
Regular, scarce, pr.	125.00 – 150.00
Sauce boat	25.00 – 30.00
Sugar bowl with lid	22.00 – 28.00
Tray with handles, 8"	28.00 – 35.00

Laughlin Art China
See Plates 378 through 409.

Plate 379: Vase, with handles, Currant, 8"	100.00 – 125.00
Plate 380: Vase, Currant, 7"	90.00 – 110.00
Plate 381: Bowl, ruffled, Currant, 2" x 10"	150.00 – 165.00
Plate, Currant, 9½"	65.00 – 75.00
Plate, scalloped, Currant, 10"	80.00 – 90.00
Plate 382: Bread tray, Fe Dora, Currant, 12½"	80.00 – 90.00
Plate 383: Covered dish, Currant	190.00 – 210.00
Plate 384: Humidor, wooden lid, Currant, 5" x 6"	200.00 – 225.00
Pitcher, bulbous, Currant, 4½" x 5"	100.00 – 125.00
Orange bowl with handles, Currant, 12"	170.00 – 190.00
Pitcher, straight sides, Currant, 6½"	120.00 – 140.00
Plate 385: Chocolate pot, Currant	260.00 – 295.00
Chocolate cup & saucer, Currant	90.00 – 110.00
Plate 386: Pitcher, Dutch Jug, Currant, 10"	150.00 – 165.00

Plate 387: Vase, Currant, 12"...190.00 – 210.00

Plate 388: Vase, with handles, Currant, 14"...300.00 – 325.00

Plate 389: Sugar basket, Golden Fleece...210.00 – 240.00
           Sugar basket, Currant...180.00 – 200.00

Plate 390: Vase, Currant, 9¾"...150.00 – 165.00
           Vase, slim form, Currant, 12"...140.00 – 155.00
           Vase, slim form, Currant, 16"...225.00 – 250.00
           Chocolate/AD pot, Currant, 10"...260.00 – 295.00

Plate 391: Bread tray, White Pets ....150.00 – 175.00

Plate 392: Pitcher, milk; White Pets..195.00 – 215.00

Plate 393: Vase, with handles, White Pets, 8"...250.00 – 275.00

Plate 394: Ewer, White Pets, 15½" ....350.00 – 425.00

Plate 395: Chocolate cup & saucer, gold trim, Flow Blue...160.00 – 180.00

Plate 396: Bonbon, gold trim, Flow Blue..160.00 – 180.00

Plate 397: Jardiniere, with handles, gold trim, Flow Blue, 10" x 14".......................600.00 – 700.00

Plate 398: Cuspidor, lady's, gold trim Flow Blue, 5½" x 8"......................................345.00 – 360.00

Plate 399 & 400: Plates, Flow Blue, each..160.00 – 180.00

Plate 401: Mug, Jacobean design ....70.00 – 85.00
           Tankard, Monk ....185.00 – 210.00
           Mug, Monk..70.00 – 85.00

Plate 402: Tankard, American Floral..345.00 – 360.00

Plate 403: Tankard, American eagle & flags ....350.00 – 380.00

Plate 404: Tankard, American Beauty..345.00 – 360.00
           Mug, American Beauty ....100.00 – 125.00

Plate 405: Bowl, lady with breasts exposed..300.00 – 350.00

Plate 406: Charger, American Beauty, 10" ....125.00 – 150.00

Plate 407: Stein, football player...300.00 – 325.00

Plate 408: Pitcher, milk; plums..130.00 – 165.00

Plate 409: Stein, advertising ....200.00 – 220.00

Additional Art China, not shown:
           Bowl, 17th-century child in center, gold trim, ruffled, Flow Blue ....160.00 – 180.00
           Bowl, lady & peacock, 9"..200.00 – 250.00
           Cake plate, with handles, Fe Dora, Currant, 10".....................................110.00 – 125.00
           Creamer (matches Currant Sugar basket)...90.00 – 110.00

Additional Art China, not shown (continued):

Creamer (matches Golden Fleece sugar basket)..100.00 – 125.00
Mug, Currant ....70.00 – 85.00
Mug, lady and peacock, woman feeding birds ....120.00 – 150.00
Orange bowl, lady and peacock, shape shown in Plate 384 ....300.00 – 325.00
Plate, Currant, 7" ....40.00 – 45.00
Plate, White Pets, child and donkey ....125.00 – 150.00
Rose bowl, Currant, 4" ....150.00 – 165.00
Stein, White Pets ....160.00 – 180.00
Tankard, Currant, shape as shown in Plate 404 ....250.00 – 300.00
Vase, lady & peacock, gold trim, 12"..345.00 – 360.00
Vase, White Pets, with cats, shape as shown in Plate 388 ....400.00 – 425.00

Dreamland

See Plates 410 through 417.

Plate 410: Stein ....160.00 – 185.00
Tankard ....250.00 – 300.00

Plate 411: Vase, 3½" ....125.00 – 150.00

Plate 412: Bowl, ruffled, 10" ....185.00 – 210.00
Jug ....185.00 – 210.00

Plate 413: Plate, closed handles, 10½" ....190.00 – 210.00

Plates 414 & 417: Plaque, 10"...170.00 – 190.00

Plate 415: Vase, 16" ....275.00 – 325.00

Plate 416: Vase, 10" ....200.00 – 225.00
Plate, open handles, 10"...190.00 – 210.00

Other Early Lines

See Plates 418 through 425.

Plate 418: Orange bowl, Laughlin's Holland..225.00 – 250.00

Plate 419: Jug, Holland, 6½"..225.00 – 250.00

Plate 420: Bowl, fruit; Empress shape, 5" ....25.00 – 35.00
Bowl, coupe, Empress shape, 8"...50.00 – 65.00
Cup, Empress shape ....30.00 – 45.00

Plate 421: Plate, Empress shape, 9" ....35.00 – 45.00

Not shown: Plate, Empress shape, 6"..25.00 – 35.00

Plate 422: Pitcher, Genesee shape, ca 1915, 3½"...90.00 – 115.00

Plates 423 & 425: Plate, Yellowstone shape, 6½"...25.00 – 35.00

Plate 424: Platter, Yellowstone shape, 9"..50.00 – 65.00

World's Fair: The American Potter
See Plates 426 through 437.

NEV = No Established Value.

Plate 426: Plate HLC World's Fair, either year ....150.00 – 200.00

Plate 427: Marmalade, complete, Edwin Knowles, very rare ....100.00 – 150.00

Plate 428: Cake set, Cronin China Co...75.00 – 85.00
Bowl, Paden City Pottery, 10" ....75.00 – 85.00
Plate, Knowles, 10¾"...100.00 – 135.00
Marmalade (see Plate 427 for complete example)
Pitcher, Porcelier ....175.00 – 250.00

Other Porcelier not shown:
Creamer ....75.00 – 100.00
Juice pitcher...135.00 – 160.00
Sugar bowl...75.00 – 100.00
Teapot, large ....220.00 – 260.00
Teapot, medium ....200.00 – 230.00
Teapot, small..250.00 – 275.00

Plate 431: Vase, 5" to 8"...125.00 – 175.00
Under 5" ....70.00 – 110.00
Candle holder, each ....75.00 – 100.00
Bowl ....100.00 – 125.00
Individual creamer ....45.00 – 55.00

Plate 429: Vase, 7"..150.00 – 175.00

Plate 430: Cup & saucer, Zodiac ....75.00 – 85.00

Plate 432: Plate, Golden Gate Expo, either year ....110.00 – 130.00
Ashtray, Golden Gate Expo ....80.00 – 90.00

Plate 433: Bowl, Four Seasons, each ....60.00 – 70.00

Plate 434 – 435: Plate, Potters; either view
Turquoise or tan ....25.00 – 35.00
Ivory or green ....65.00 – 80.00
Box only ....40.00 – 50.00

Plate 436: Pitcher, Martha Washington, ivory, 5"..60.00 – 70.00

Plate 437: Pitchers, George and Martha Washington, cobalt, 5" ....NEV

Miscellaneous

See Plates 438 through 446.

NEV = No Established Value.

Plate 438: Sit 'n Sip, see Commercial Adaptations for pricing information.

Plate 439: Tom & Jerry bowl..50.00 – 60.00
              Tom & Jerry mug..10.00 – 15.00.

Plate 440: Nude vase ....350.00 – 385.00
              Donkey ashtray..500.00 – 530.00

Plate 441: Bill Booth football ....900.00 – 1,100.00

Plate 442: Chip & dip, 12" ....NEV

Plate 443: Leaf saucers, 7"..NEV

Values for Our Early Editions

The earlier editions of our Fiesta book have themselves become sought-after collectibles. Remember that condition is important, and values are given for copies in very fine condition.

First Edition ....150.00 – 200.00
Second Editon ....85.00 – 100.00
Third Edition..65.00 – 75.00
Fourth Edition..40.00 – 50.00
Fifth Edition..25.00 – 30.00